LEADERSHIP

Leadership

THE ESSENTIAL COMPETENCIES FOR THE 21ST CENTURY

Dr. Guy M. Ngayo Fotso

Vertica Publishing

First Printing, 2021

Prepared for publication by Cilaine Maurin
Cover Design by Julia Ruiz
Illustrations by Floriane Ryan

ISBN 9782957870806 (paperback)
ISBN 9782957870820 (hardcover)

Published by Vertica Publishing

18 ESSENTIAL COMPETENCIES FOR THE 21ST CENTURY

Which Are You Missing?

Revisit nine classic leadership competencies that have been around forever and need to be reshaped, and discover nine new essential competencies for the 21st century to transform yourself as a leader for our time.

A leader is...

Amaryllis (18), Niels Alexandre (15), and Giulia (14)

Leadership is...

Love and Creativity

Malena (5)

"It is not the strongest of the species that survives, nor the most intelligent that survives. It is the one that is most adaptable to change."

- Charles Darwin

Contents

Introduction

Digital transformation, globalization, millennials, sustainability, and information communication technologies are just a few of the key words associated with the unprecedented change we see in our world today and significantly affect how leadership should be conducted.

The concept of leadership was introduced to me as a child when I was observing my parents, both of them serial entrepreneurs. My father, who was also a political figure, always impressed me with his ability to inspire others and get people to follow him and his ideas. He was very influential and extremely charismatic. He had amazing cognitive abilities, was a fast strategic thinker, and very good at solving problems. People liked him but also feared him. His leadership style was rather authoritative, directive, and very much top-down. My mother, on the other hand, was very successful and delivered great results using a different approach to leadership. Her leadership style was much more collaborative, moving in the direction of laissez-faire appealing to people's self-responsibility. People who worked for her were free to try and implement initiatives they believed could be beneficial to her various small enterprises. She was a trustworthy leader, whom most of her business partners, peers, and employees liked because of her natural pleasantness and ability to create an enjoyable environment based on trust and authenticity.

After being exposed to different leadership styles from kindergarten to high school, in different sport clubs and performing arts projects, I later attended business school, where I found myself surrounded by many other students, most of them aspiring to become the next big leaders. It seemed as if every single one us believed we had something special that was going to make us stand out from the crowd and become influential public figures. All of us wanted to become leaders without really knowing what it meant, besides being the heroic person in charge. We all believed that business school would give us the tools and develop us all into great leaders. Today, it actually makes me smile.

Several years down the road, we all ended up in careers where we had to manage teams, deal with meeting objectives, cope with complex situations, as well as organize, plan, budget, supervise, and solve problems. All these tasks fall into what Kotter (1987) defines "as the management process—they stand in contrast with the performance that would be expected from a leader." As students, we found it hard to understand that business school had failed in making us leaders but had instead equipped us with the set of skills and tools to make us good managers.

During my career, especially after earning my MBA, I went through several leadership development programs in a number of organizations. All of the programs had different approaches, concepts, and durations running from two days to two weeks of intensive study. During the seminars, we had several personality tests, team building activities, and strategic workshops. Most of the time we ended up with great ideas, great initiatives, and action plans to improve our leadership skills and our teams' performance. However, after several days, all was forgotten and we fell back to our previous patterns and habits. Unfortunately, we did not show much development in our leadership skills.

After several years of observing how I have developed as a leader, I started to question the various trainings I had attended. Why did I feel they did not really contribute to helping me develop my leadership skills? In my quest, I encountered several peer-reviewed scientific research articles and comments in popular press and magazines, all of them casting serious doubts about the quality and efficiency of most of the currently available leadership training programs, even those delivered by highly prestigious and well-respected training organizations. Most of the published documents claimed that existing leadership training programs fail at developing leaders because of three main reasons: they are too short to actually change behaviors and patterns, the training methods used are not adapted for leadership development, or the wrong profiles are sent to these trainings and most people attending are not intrinsically motivated and felt forced to attend. The general agreed consensus that strikes me the most was the idea that most leadership trainings do not focus on developing the right leadership skills. Surprisingly, despite a high level of dissatisfaction around leadership training programs, organizations are still dedicating a high percentage of their training budget to leadership development. One may ask, "why are organizations still investing so much in leadership development?" An obvious reason is because leadership is essential for the successes and failures of organizations. Second, it is based on the assumption that leadership can be trained and leadership requirements evolve to adapt to a constantly changing world.

As I started reading published peer-reviewed articles and books to identify the "right" leadership skills for our times, I quickly realized that it would require a large amount of time, effort, motivation, and dedication to come to terms with my quest because of the abundance of publications on the subject that lack consensus on the number of skills, the type of skills, and the vocabulary used to describe the skills. In some cases, different terms are used to describe the same skills. All these new publications are adding more confusion than clarity on the subject.

Therefore, I decided to commit myself to investigating what leadership competencies for the 21st century are, and to dedicate myself to shedding more light on how these can be taught.

This book is the conclusion of years of extensive scientific research work on the topic of leadership and the required leadership competencies for the 21st century. It starts by trying to answer two key questions: What is leadership? Are leaders born or made? Then, readers have the opportunity to understand the history of the most relevant leadership theories up to now and how they have evolved to match our changing world shaped by new information communication technologies, digitalization, internationalization, and cultural and demographic shifts, to name a few examples. After setting the stage with definitions and the-ories, the book focuses on the 18 required leadership competencies for the 21st century and provides insights on how to develop and train these competencies.

1

What is Leadership?

Before we start our journey on leadership competencies for the 21st century, it is essential to first define what leadership is. Such an endeavor requires us to step away from sceptics, well represented by the anti-leadership theorists, who believed there is no such thing as leadership and claim it is just a social construct. For now, let us agree that leadership is a real phenomenon.

The first attempts to define leadership in the Western World can be traced to Athenian and Greek philosophers such as Herodotus, Plato, and Aristotle. It was also an important topic for renowned thinkers the likes of Machiavelli. These great thinkers did not all provide a definition of leadership but instead listed essential personal qualities that define a leader, such as virtuosity, eagerness to serve and look after others, wisdom, intelligence, and having people's support.

Interestingly, there are now as many definitions of leadership as people who will be asked to define it. Everyone has an opinion. The question "What is leadership?" often results in never-ending debates that rarely lead to satisfying conclusions. The debate reaches beyond conversations in boardrooms and break rooms, with even highly respected leadership academics discussing and considering the question. So, where do we start?

To search for an agreed upon definition of leadership is to embark on a historical journey in a field where the first research papers were published as early as the 19th century. Through the course of history, leadership has been studied in different fields and from various perspectives, such as cross-cultural leadership, political leadership, and social psychology, among others. As we make our way through the centuries worth of sources, it may be time to face the brutal fact that there are too many different definitions of leadership.

Iles and Preece (2006) define leadership by distancing it from management, suggesting the following: "whereas managers are concerned with today, with delivery, targets, efficiency, utilization, and authority, focusing on internal organizational issues, on control and on doing things right, leaders are held to be oriented to tomorrow, to development, to direction, to purpose and vision, and to innovation" (p. 319). Meanwhile, Northhouse (2010) suggests another perspective by explaining that: "Leadership is a process whereby an individual influences a group of individuals to achieve a common goal" (p 3). Further, Stogdill (1974) provides a third varying perspective, stating: "Leadership is the initiation and maintenance of structure in expectation and interaction" (p.411).

Considering even just these three definitions from a myriad of others, we can see the scope of different interpretations explored by scholars. When taking into account the immense number of available sources on leadership and the diverse definitions they provide, it seems impossible to come up with a single ideal definition. In fact, there is little optimism that a single, undisputed definition can or will be published in the future. Attempts to find a unified definition are further complicated by the shift in the mindset of leadership academics over the years from an authoritative perspective to one more focused on influence. Due to this ideological shift, finding a definition of leadership that fits everyone is out of the question.

While reaching a single definition may be unfeasible, what is possible is providing a basic view of leadership by finding the generally agreed upon points from the numerous divergent definitions available today. Based on my research, I have found there is a common consensus on these seven key points:

- Leadership is a dynamic process.
- A leader can be one or more people (team leadership).
- The process involves at least two people: a leader and a follower.
- It is a process of influence. The follower must be free and willing to follow. Any case in which force or coercive measures are used or an individual loses their free will is no longer considered as a form of leadership.
- There must be a goal to reach.
- Followers should be trained and well-equipped to accomplish their tasks.
- A leader shares the vision and sets the example.

Even with these key principles, a question that often comes up is whether there is a difference between leadership and management. It may be tempting to argue that actually there is none because leaders also need to manage activities until accomplishment and the end-result is achieved. Vice versa, managers also somehow need to lead people to get them do things. This argument is clearly valid. Leaders need to demonstrate some skills often associated to managers, such as organizational skills to provide structure (planning, defining roles and responsibilities, setting objectives, providing feedback). To get things done, managers often rely on a range of different leadership styles, such as authoritative, collaborative, or laissez-faire.

Great minds in the field of leadership, however, tend to agree that there is a clear difference between leaders and managers, regardless of the competencies they have in common. The difference is grounded on what they *mostly* focus on. This is very much expressed by Kotter (1998) when he argues that managers focus more on handling complexity by instituting planning and budgeting, organizing and staffing, and controlling and problem solving, whereas leaders spend more time handling change, setting direction, aligning, empowering, motivating, and inspiring people. In addition, managers will tend to focus on control, scope reduction, and limiting choices, and can often rely on coercion and authority, while leaders will tend to consider different possible alternatives, look at the long-term vision, change people's attitudes, and rely on influence rather than authority.

Since our current society tends to value leadership over management, there is a great pressure to turn everyone into leaders or for everyone to appear as a leader. However, this is not really necessary since both managers and leaders are needed and are equally important-they are complementary. Being in a leadership role should be a question of personal decision. No one should be forced nor pushed into that role if they have no interest in it. Now, reading this, you may want to ask: if you are a natural born leader, is leadership still a choice?

Well, that is a great question. Is there really something as a natural born leader? The chapter that follows attempts to answer the still vivid question: are leaders born or made?

2

Are Leaders Born or Made?

Once a debate on the definition of leadership has subsided, another often follows regarding the question of whether leaders are born or made. From my experience, the rooms in which these heated debates unfold very often end up divided, with a group believing leaders are born, another group insisting they are made, and a third group saying they are both born and made. Convincing anyone to change their opinion is often a challenge. An inability to convince or be convinced leaves the room divided with no consensus. The question is, who is right? Hard to say. The discussion around this topic is nothing new, it has existed since the beginning of the science of leadership. In the following chapter, I hope to bring some clarity to the debate. I don't intend to give a definite answer but rather to provide a different perspective by bringing together knowledge from different schools of thought.

To answer the question at hand, it is first important to determine whether there can be such a thing as a natural leader. Is leadership a part of human nature? Is there even such a thing as human nature? What is human nature? These are difficult questions to answer as there have been numerous different perspectives born from economics, politics, psychology, and sociology. Each of these disciplines needs to define human nature in order to develop theories that are related and applicable to their fields. However, the first debates on human nature are rooted in philosophy, where varying views on the subject cohabit. While Thomas Hobbes stressed a very negative perspective of human nature, Jean-Jacques Rousseau expressed the positive nature of human beings. René Descartes and Immanuel Kant saw human beings as neither negative nor positive by nature, but rather driven by passion. Before all of them, Aristotle defined human beings as social and rational animals. In consequence, how can we define human nature?

In the quest to find definitions for complex phenomena, such as leadership or human nature, it is often easier to break them down into smaller parts. To define human nature is to identify specific human characteristics, which should be shared by all human beings, with no exceptions. Emmanuel Levinas provided an element of an answer by focusing on the physical aspects of humans. In his philosophy, he stressed the importance of the face as a key element in recognizing other human beings. Contemplating Levinas' focus on the physical leads us to consider the science of genetics and the fact that there is a human genome encoded as DNA. *All* human beings share this "homo sapiens" genome. Human DNA is composed of about 21,000 genes, which are responsible for the development of the human body. Twenty-three pairs of chromosomes are needed for human DNA. Even if we all share the same genome, each of us has a unique genetic code expressed through the DNA in our cells, hormones, and brain, which, in turn, influence our behavior, temperament, and experiences. So, we are not completely blank from birth, as Steven Pinker claims in his book from 2003.

At birth, every human receives 50% of their DNA from each parent, with a copy of each gene coming from the two parents. Each parent has two separate copies of an allele at every location on the chromosome. Therefore, if two parents who are great leaders have a child, there is no guarantee they will inherit the "leadership gene." Even if we were to assume that the child would, in fact, inherit the "leadership gene", through their research on identical twins, researchers in the field of epigenetics have proved that it may not be that simple. Identical twins who share the same genotype can potentially develop different phenotypes. This is due to modifications that can occur in the chromosome and influences from environmental factors, which can impact either gene activation or gene repression. The phenomenon, known as the DNA methylation process, takes place when mutated groups are added to DNA molecules and contribute to the repression of gene transcription.

A study on identical twins confirmed the importance of how external environments, such as our social environment, influence our genes. Furthermore, from the perspective of behavioral genetics, it is also necessary to consider how the environment within the body can impact our genes. Interaction with other genes, hormones, cells, and tissues can also impact the expression or repression of a gene. In addition, both biopsychology and behavioral genetics have shown that most traits are polygenetic, which means that several genes need to interact with each other in order for a trait to emerge. This finding clarifies that it is not only one gene, but rather several genes interacting cooperatively, that leads to a trait developing in a person. So, in fact, inheriting a "leadership gene" would not lead you to develop leadership traits.

Perhaps the debate on whether leaders are born or made could be settled if an actual "leadership gene" had been discovered. Thus far, despite the plethora of studies attempting to identify the magical "leadership gene," none have been conclusive. The most significant result has been research showing that dopamine, a neurotransmitter present in the body, plays a role in influencing motivation, impulsivity, and self-regulation, which are all important elements of leadership. Looking further, two significant studies have attempted to discover a leadership gene after discovering potential direct links between the found genes and leadership. In the first study, the researchers aimed to identify the DAT1 10 repeat allele, while in the second study, the researchers investigating the gene rs4950 SNP failed to demonstrate a direct link between the discovered genes and leadership. In fact, both studies recognized the important role played by the environment.

These findings prove that there is no proof or research that confirms there is a gene for leadership. Becoming a leader is not as easy as simply inheriting or being born with a "leadership gene"; rather, it is a complex phenomenon, based on external and internal factors, in which many things have to take place to allow for the expression of that gene. So far, however, no gene has been found to be determinant in leadership expression.

At this point, you may be thinking, "Well, if no peer reviewed or serious publication has confirmed the existence of a leadership gene, then leaders are not born, and therefore, must be made." However, the debate continues. Since there are other proven examples of personality traits, like cognitive ability or Erik Erikson's big five personality traits, both of which are influenced by a person's genes and can be inherited through their parents, we can't completely overlook the impact of genes on leadership development. Depending on who you refer to, the impact of genes on leadership ability is estimated to be between 25%-30%. This suggests we should not underestimate the impact that our genes may have for the emergence of leadership qualities or traits, even if it is difficult to measure exactly how responsible they are.

The conclusion that leaders are more likely made than born is one that is shared among many philosophers. Erasmus said, "Man is certainly not born but made man." He stressed the importance of education for people's development. Rousseau, as well as many others, also insisted on the important role education has in our development. These philosophers considered education within the social context. As human beings, we need to live in groups in order to ensure survival and adapt to our environments, a concept specified by Aristotle. By living in a group, people share a culture in the form of their beliefs, values, norms, symbols, and languages. That culture is transmitted through the process of socialization at a very young age. This indicates the fact that leadership is cultural. What one culture may perceive as leadership may not be leadership in the eyes of another. This element of culture, which influences how people behave, is created collectively by the members of a social group and does not emerge through a biological process. Many behaviorist philosophers believe in the impact of a person's social environment and shared culture on their behavior. They believe the environment is responsible for people's behavior and that it affects their personality development. Freud, Adler, Erikson, Jung, and Piaget all stressed the importance of the social environment in shaping personality. In the philosophy of Neo-Freudism, this development is fixed at an early stage of life, while for most others, it occurs throughout a person's lifetime.

Consequently, it is fair to argue that a leader's development starts at a very young age and continues throughout their life as their personality evolves due to constant interpersonal interactions, challenges faced, and experiences gained.

So, are leaders born or made? There is still room to debate this question, but what we can see from the countless philosophers and scientists who have taken on the question, for the time being, it seems that although leaders can be influenced by genetics, they are also massively affected by their social environments, culture, and experiences. There is still room for further discoveries on how exactly our genes affect leadership abilities, and perhaps more clarity will be found in the future, which makes it hard to totally rule out the effect of genes on leadership. As of now, research has come to the conclusion that leadership might be influenced by our genes in the range of 5% to 20%, and that the remaining influence (80% to 95%) comes from education and training. However, the rate suggested between genes and training influences varies from scientist to scientist; therefore, a general agreement is yet to be reached.

Having come to this conclusion, we can move on to investigate and contemplate how the views and theories on leadership have changed throughout history and how it is seen today.

3

Traditional Leadership Theories

The concept of leaders and leadership has existed for a very long time. Philosophers and scientists throughout the ages have proposed theories of what makes a good leader, how they should lead, and what their ideal competencies and traits should be. To consider leadership in the future, we need to understand what people believed in the past. In the next two chapters, I will introduce several theories on leadership from the past and the present. The theories have been categorized as either traditional or contemporary.

The following traditional theories of leadership were developed through the 19th and 20th centuries and were among the first theories to consider the question of leadership. Many of these theories have been revised by theorists in the 21st century, who have either added to or argued against certain aspects of the theories.

The Great Man Theory
19th Century (1840s-1880s)

Major Theorists: Thomas Carlyle (1841), Francis Galton (1870), William James (1880)

The main idea behind this theory is that the world has been shaped by "great men" who were born with qualities that allowed them to be exceptional individuals. Having these qualities gave them the ability to achieve social change, something "ordinary" people could not do. The theory advocates that each great leader is born already possessing the traits that would allow them to rise and lead. Their ability to lead is instinctual and activated when their surroundings require it. The great man theory can easily be imagined by thinking of the archetypical hero who rises when adversity requires. They do it for the well-being of others to either enlighten them or restore order and bring new perspectives. Theorists of the time were inspired by Charles Darwin, believing that the "great man's" exceptional qualities were transmitted from generation to generation. Great man theorists, like Galton, distinguished between hereditary genius and ability: abilities can be learned but very quickly lost if not used or trained, whereas hereditary genius qualities will always be present even without extensive training. In their minds, the hereditary genius of a leader would always be present, making it more desirable, even if they were not trained. Those who trained as leaders could easily lose their abilities and were therefore not as strong. However, an exceptional individual is not the only factor at play in the great man theory. Indeed, the key to these "great men" becoming leaders is their environment. To successfully bring about social change, their inherent talents must be aligned with the needs of their surroundings. As the world changes and our environment changes, different talents and gifts are necessary; therefore, a "great man" can only rise only when their particular hereditary genius is required and fits a specific context.

The Trait Theory
20th Century (1920s -1950s)

Major Theorists: Edward L. Munson (1921), A.O Bowden (1926), Floyd H. Allport (1926), W.V Bingham (1927), C. Schenk (1928), J.B Nash (1929), Ralph M. Stogdill (1948)

21st Century Theorists: House (1988), Smith, Martorana and, Owens (2003), Atonakis, Day and Schyns (2012)

Following the great man theory, philosophers began to consider the trait theory. Rather than believing that heroes appeared in times of need, having been born for the moment, trait theorists took a slightly more practical approach. They considered there were specific critical traits that allowed individuals to emerge as leaders, and that by defining these skills and traits, people could be selected for leadership positions. One of the theorists, Ralph Stoghill, was the first to attempt to compile a list of possible traits a leader should possess. In 1974 he published his list of leadership traits and skills.

Traits: Adaptable to situations | Alert to social environment | Ambitious and achievement-oriented | Assertive | Cooperative, Decisive | Dependable, Dominant (desire to influence others) | Energetic (high activity level) | Persistent | Self-confident | Tolerant of stress | Willing to assume responsibility.

Skills: Clever (intelligent) | Conceptually skilled | Creative | Diplomatic and tactful | Fluent in speaking | Knowledgeable about group tasks | Organized (administrative ability) | Persuasive | Socially skilled

While this may have been a step away from the great man theory, it was still met with criticism. Possessing the traits on Stoghills' list did not guarantee a good leader in every situation. Some of the listed traits may also be highly dependent on the group of people the leader is attempting to lead. The listed traits also continue to describe someone of a generally extroverted nature (socially skilled, self-confident, energetic, etc.), not quite leaving behind the classic idea of the charismatic "great man," when, in fact, introverts can also be highly effective leaders. One of the main criticisms of the trait theory was that even if an individual possessed these necessary traits and skills to *emerge* as a leader, it would not be enough to guarantee that they would in fact be an *effective* leader.

Despite its criticism, the trait theory has not been completely cast aside. The inborn qualities of a leader continued to be discussed throughout the 20th century, and even today, theorists contemplate the revival of the trait theory of leadership.

The Power and Influence Theory
20th Century (1950s-1980s)

Major Theorists: Schenk (1928), French & Raven (1959), Kipnis & Schmidt (1983)

21st Century Theorists: Lee, Han, Cheong, Kim, and Yun (2017)

The great man theory and the trait theory both depend on the existence of a somewhat extraordinary individual. The power and influence theory distinguishes itself from these previous leadership theories by recognizing that leadership is linked to something more than a singular "hero." It is based on the relationship between individuals. The theory suggests that leaders can use their power and influence to lead others and achieve their desired outcomes. Two of the most influential theorists, French and Raven, identified six sources of power that a leader can use to influence others: legitimate, reward, coercive, expert, referent, and informational. They believed that a leader stood in a solid position of power and that any strategy they chose to use, even coercion, was an acceptable way to deal with others. However, this belief was not shared by all power and influence theorists. Persuasion, influence, and inspiration were often considered better ways of leading others. In fact, the idea of power as the sole notion of influence was critiqued. As the theory evolved, persuasion and influence became the center. Power and influence theorists expanded their beliefs to include the idea that the opinions, interests, and will of subordinates should be taken into consideration by a leader. A more contemporary approach to the power and influence theory identifies a set of six highly effective influence tactics: rational persuasion, inspiration appeal, apprising, collaboration, ingratiation, and consultation.

Behavioral Theory
20th Century (1930s - 1960s)

Major Theorists: Lewin, Lippit, and White (1939), Shartle (1956), Stogdill & Coons (1957), McGregor (1960), Rensis Likert (1961), Robert Blake & Jane Mouton (1964)

Another leadership theory that emerged in the mid-20th century was the behavioral theory. The behavioral theory demonstrated that most of the trait-based leadership theories were not conclusive since a set of traits or qualities shared by all effective leaders is difficult to identify. Rather than focus on who the leader is, behavioral theorists focused on what a leader does, as well as their observable behaviors. Unlike the great man and trait theory, the behavioral theory posits that leadership can be taught. It is diverse in its different perspectives and truly seeks to uncover a leader's attitudes and behaviors towards their subordinates.

The theory was developed in part due to experimental studies of group life, through which three leadership styles were identified, each with associated behaviors: autocratic, democratic, and laissez-faire. In auto-cratic leadership, subordinates are not consulted by the leader in decision making, unlike the democratic style, where the leader takes into consideration the perspectives of their subordinates in order to reach a consensus. The laissez-faire style involves little participation from the leader at all. A key idea of the behavioral theory is that there is no perfect style as they each have pros and cons. An autocratic leadership style may lead to a feeling of restraint and frustration, a democratic style can be counter-productive if too many diverse opinions are expressed when trying to reach an agreement, and a laissez-faire style can lead to a lack of coherence and guidance, leaving subordinates feeling frustrated and dissatisfied with their own work. The appropriate style of leadership should be adapted to the subordinates and to various environments. That being said, the democratic style is often preferred as it leads to less hostility, aggression, and apathy, while still offering guidance and purpose.

In the late 1950s, the leader behavior description questionnaire (LBDQ) was created as a way to allow subordinates to identify their leader's behavior. The questionnaire targeted two dimensions: the leader's level of consideration and the leader's desire to initiate structure. Essentially, subordinates are asked to consider the extent to which their leader pays attention to their needs and feelings. A leader with high consideration will foster human relationships and rely on trust. On the other hand, a leader with an initiating structure approach tends to show more control over tasks and subordinates by focusing on defining clear roles and responsibilities and setting operating procedures. The study developed from the questionnaire concluded that a successful leader should be balanced, try to be close to and attentive to the needs of their subordinates, and be able to provide structure by defining clear roles and goals.

Around the same time, researchers were also exploring alternative theories in attempts to define the dimensions of a successful and effective leader. Rensis Likert considered leadership through the lens of two orientations that impact productivity and job satisfaction: the orientation toward employees and the orientation toward production. On one side, the employee-oriented leader focuses on interpersonal relationships, listens to the employees' concerns, and becomes closer to them, much like the LBDQ's leader with high consideration. On the other side, production-oriented leaders focus more on the task at hand, the result, and the performance of employees, which is closer to the LB-DQs initiating structure approach. However, Likert's studies had more definitive results and showed that leaders who focused more on their employees achieved better outcomes. From these results, Likert developed his "four systems" of management: exploitative authority, benevolent authority, consultative, and participative. He defined exploitative authority as a system where those in the highest level of the hierarchy take full responsibility and impose decisions onto their subordinates. In benevolent authority, managers still shoulder the responsibilities, but they will use some rewards to stimulate subordinates' motivation. A change takes place with the consultative system, where leaders take into consideration the subordinate's point of view. There is more interaction, more communication, and a greater sense of teamwork in comparison to the first two systems. Finally, in the participative system, everyone, both subordinates and leaders, feel equally responsible for the work. Teamwork and participation are highly valued, and confidence and trust exist between subordinates and leaders. Likert proved that the consultative and the participative systems generated better performance than the first two. In fact, the participative system had the best results overall.

Digging deeper into the behavioral theory of leadership, theorists have considered how leaders can be influenced by their assumptions of their subordinates' attitudes at work. McGregor, in particular, coined the notions of theory X and theory Y leaders. Theory X leaders tend to use autocratic leadership styles (coercion, control, little exchange) because they have a pessimistic view of their subordinates at work, believing they don't like to work and will avoid working when possible. On the other hand, theory Y type leaders tend to apply a participative style (more exchange, more trust, more teamwork) as they have a positive opinion of their subordinates at work, assuming they enjoy working, that they want to contribute to the organization's overall objective, and that they are self-driven.

Other significant contributors to the behavioral leadership theory are Robert Blake and Jane Mouton. Building on the work of previous theorists, they proposed what came to be called a "managerial grid" designed around two variables: the concern for people (the extent to which the leader cares about the well-being of the people they directly supervise) and the concern for production (the level of importance that the leader places on results and task accomplishment). For this grid, Blake and Mouton suggested five leadership styles: country club management style (high concern for people, little concern for results), impoverished management (little concern for people and results), the authority obedience style (little concern for people, high concern for results), organization man management (searching for a compromise between concern for people and concern for results), and team management (attempts to optimize concern for people and concern for results). A leader's choice of style will ultimately depend on their concern for people and for results, applying the style that can best achieve their goals.

Blake and Mouton suggested that leaders should aim for the team management style as it generates the best performance, once again calling for a balanced leader.

The behavioral theory, in all its shapes, primarily focuses on the balance between people and results, and empathy and control. Most behavioral theorists agree that a balanced leader (one that can prioritize their relationships with subordinates while also motivating them for high results) will succeed in achieving the best performance.

Contingency Theory
20th Century (1960s - 1970s)

Major Theorists: Fiedler (1964), Hersey & Blanchard (1969), House (1970), Tannenbaum & Schmidt (1975)

The behavioral theory made several strides in considering two critical parameters, a leader's orientation towards people, and their orientation towards production. Building on that, the contingency theory explains that there is no one best leadership style that is effective in all situations, but rather that leaders should apply a style that best suits the situation. In addition, contingency theorists believe that a leader can be trained to improve in styles or situations they do not feel comfortable with.

Fiedler, who was considered the pioneer of the contingency theory, defined three situations that could influence a leaders' efficiency, thus building on the task orientation and the relationship orientation of a leader developed by the behaviorists. The three situations are created by combining three variables:

1. Leader-member relations: to what extent do the leader and the subordinates have a good relationship?
2. Task structure: the degree to which the job is structured, ranging from highly to poorly structured.
3. Position of power: the level of authority the leader has.

Combining these three variables, the following three situations are generated:

1. Favorable situation: all three variables are in the high range.
2. Intermediate favorable situation: some variables are in the poor or low range and others are in the good or high range.
3. Unfavorable situation: all three variables are in the low range.

Fiedler agreed with the behaviorists that leaders could not change their own style as it was rooted in their orientation towards either relationships or tasks. However, he also believed that leaders should be placed in situations that best fit their leadership styles. If an ideal placement is not possible, a leader can be trained to adapt his or her style to the situation. Ideally, the task-oriented leader would be placed in favorable and unfavorable situations, while the relationship-oriented leader would be best in any of the situations.

Following in Fiedler's footsteps, Hersey and Blanchard developed a situational leadership approach in the late 70s by revisiting some of their previous work on the life cycle theory of leadership. They built their theory around three main parameters. First, they relied on leader behavior orientation toward initiating structure or toward consideration for people. With these two variables, four leadership styles are described:

1. Telling (Directing)
2. Selling (Coaching)
3. Participating (Supporting)

4. Delegating (give full responsibility to the subordinates for some part of the work)

Second, they believed the maturity level of the subordinates would be the driving factor to identify the appropriate leadership style to fit the situation. A subordinate's level of maturity is essentially defined as their level of experience and performance in their jobs, as well as their willingness to be independent and to take on responsibilities. Four levels of maturity are identified:

- Maturity level 1: little competence and not willing to do the task.
- Maturity level 2: unable to do the task but willing to do it.
- Maturity level 3: competent for the task but lack the confidence to do it.
- Maturity level 4: very capable of doing the task, willing to do it, and ready to do it.

Considering the four leadership styles and the four levels of maturity of the subordinates they categorized, Hersey and Blanchard then generated the following combinations:

1. The leadership style of **telling** is best suited with **maturity level 1** subordinates.
2. The leadership style of **selling** works best with **maturity level 2** subordinates.
3. The leadership style of **participating** is more appropriate for **maturity level 3** subordinates.
4. The leadership style of **delegating** best fits **maturity level 4** subordinates.

The contingency theorists did not stop there. Two additional theorists, Tannenbaum and Schmidt, developed the leadership continuum. They agreed that a leader's behavior is influenced by their orientation either towards tasks (autocratic style) or people (democratic style). However, they also believed that leaders should be flexible enough to adapt as the level of maturity of their subordinates increases and to any time constraint or pressure. They proposed a continuum that goes from fully autocratic to fully democratic, along which leaders can move back and forth depending on the level of freedom they want to give to subordinates. To make it applicable, they suggested seven different behaviors along the continuum:

1. Manager makes decision and announces it (fully autocratic).
2. Manager "sells" decision (selling).
3. Manager presents idea and invites questions.
4. Manager presents tentative decision subject to change.
5. Manager presents problems, gets suggestions, and makes decisions.
6. Manager defines limits, asks group to make decisions.
7. Manager permits subordinates to function within the limits defined by superiors (democratic).

Finally, and of considerable importance to the contingency theory, is the path-goal theory developed by House. The theory was based primarily on the expectancy theory, which assumes that it is possible to predict people's behaviors and attitudes in regard to the expectations they have, as well as the satisfaction and value perceived from the outcome of their behaviors. From the path-goal theory perspective, the leader's behavior influences the level of performance of their subordinates. It has an impact on subordinates' perceptions of how attractive the goals are and how to achieve those goals. The greater a leader's ability to make goals attractive and clear, the more positive influence they have on their subordinates' level of satisfaction, performance, and leader acceptance. The leader's behaviors and their impact on their subordinates are dependent on two contingent variables: the personal characteristics of the subordinates and the environmental pressure.

1. Personal Characteristics of the subordinates includes:
   ○ Level of acceptance of authority: to what extent the subordinates like to be told what to do.
   ○ Locus of control: the extent to which the subordinates believe they have control over the goals.
   ○ Perception of ability: how much the subordinates believe they have the ability to do the tasks.
2. External pressure includes:
   ○ Subordinate tasks and characteristics: level of repetitiveness of the tasks.
   ○ Formal authority system: the degree of a leader's position of power.
   ○ Primary workgroup: the relationship between subordinates.

Drawing from these variables, House developed 4 leadership styles:

1. Supportive: it should have a good impact on subordinates' performance and satisfaction. It fits best when subordinates are experiencing stress, frustration, and dissatisfaction with the job to be done.
2. Achievement-oriented: will get the subordinates to strive for better performance and boosts their confidence in the ability to do the job: This style is supposed to be very efficient when the subordinates have to deal with ambiguous and non-repetitive tasks or moderate unambiguous and repetitive tasks.
3. Participative: this style is appropriate when subordinates have a high confidence in their ability to do the job and they believe they have a lot of control over the tasks to be done; for example, by being able to choose what tasks they want to do. The participative style should then lead to greater satisfaction and greater performance.
4. Directive: by applying this style, the leader is expected to compensate for the lack of organizational structure and clarity of the

tasks. Therefore, it is supposed to be effective when an organization has failed to provide clear rules and policies and when the tasks to be done are either repetitive and unambiguous or non-routine and ambiguous.

Transactional Leadership Theory
20th Century (1940s - 1980s)

Major Theorists: Max Weber (1947), Graen & Hollander (1958), Cashman (1975), Liden & Hoel (1982), Kellerman (1984), Bass (1985), Kuhnert & Lewis (1987)

21st Century Theorists: Lunenburg (2010), Malos (2012), McCleskey (2014)

The transactional leadership style is based on the principle that a leader and their followers engage in a mutually dependent relationship. It is also sometimes referred to as the management theory of leadership. Within the theory, the leader provides their subordinates with something of value to them, and in return, receives, from the subordinates, something they want. This is also described as the principle of reciprocal influence. Leaders and their subordinates can exchange material things (e.g., a signed work contract) as well as social things (e.g., emotional support). Some theorists have distinguished between two elements of transactions: the high-quality level related to interpersonal relationships and the low-quality level linked to goods and rights. Of course, higher quality transactions generate better performance. In this theory, the effectiveness of the leader will depend on their ability to adapt and match what they have to exchange with the constantly changing needs and expectations of their subordinates.

Another key element to the success of a leader applying the transactional leadership style is to clearly define roles and responsibilities. During the "role-making process," leaders first have to be recognized and accepted by their subordinates. This requires meeting their expectations to accumulate credit. The more credit accumulated, the greater influence the leader has over their subordinates.

Some defined characteristics of a transactional leader are as follows:

- Contingent reward: contracts exchange of rewards for effort, promises rewards for good performance, recognizes accomplishments.
- Management by exception (active): watches and searches for deviations from rules and standards, takes corrective action.
- Management by exception (passive): intervenes only if standards are not met.
- Laissez-faire: abdicates responsibilities, avoids making decisions.

Anti-Leadership Theory
20th Century (1970s - 1980s)

Major Theorists: Kerr (1977), Pfeffer (1977), Howell & Dorfman (1981), McElroy (1982)

The late 1970s marked the emergence of a new theory, which, instead of searching for characteristics, questioned the entire concept of leadership. The anti-leadership theory advocated that leadership was both a myth and a social construct. They believed that since people have a need to explain things around them they tried to develop a rational explanation for this "leadership" phenomenon they observe. However, in the minds of anti-leadership theorists, leaders become leaders because other people decide to see them as such. The traits and behaviors observed have nothing to do with it. This theory attempted to explain the failures of leadership and expanded to reject the idea that any hierarchical leadership is needed to ensure subordinates' satisfaction and success in performing tasks. The theory also states that subordinates themselves could replace leaders by considering the following:

- The degree of professionalism linked to the expertise of the subordinates, training, and task-provided feedback.
- The presence of a closely-knit cohesive workgroup.
- The degree of organization, formalization with clear written job goals, clear responsibilities, clear appraisals, and work schedule.
- The existence of unambiguous, routine, and methodological invariant tasks.

Culture-Related Leadership Theory 20th Century (1980s - 1990s)

Major Theorists: Peters & Waterman (1982), Ouchi (1982, 1993), Marz & Sims (1991)

21st Century Theorists: Dahlgaard-Park & Dahlgaard (2006), Lunenberg (2011), Schein (2011)

Based on the notion that an organization's culture has an important impact on its performance, the culture-related theory emerged closely after the anti-leadership theory. An organization's culture is based on a set of shared values, beliefs, and norms that are learned by its members. It shapes the way people behave within their chosen organization. One of the main ways culture is transmitted to new employees is through a leader's participation, behavior, and the reward system they use. The theory exists with three mains schools of thought: the search of excellence developed by Peters and Waterman, Ouchi's theory of Z, and the superleadership concept designed by Marz and Sims.

The search of excellence was developed based on the Pascale and Athos' 7S framework, with the conclusion that the best-performing companies in terms of innovation demonstrated the following eight characteristics:

1. Bias for action: experimentation is key.
2. Close to the customer: listen to and apply customers' points of view.
3. Autonomy and entrepreneurship: everyone in the organization should be creative.
4. Productivity through people: always look for ways to boost productivity and reduce waste.
5. Hands-on, value-driven: vision and mission should guide decision-making and actions.
6. Stick to the knitting: focus on core competencies.
7. Simple form, lean staff: search for simple structure.
8. Simultaneous loose-tight properties: apply centralized and decentralized at the same time.

The second of the main schools of thought, Ouchi's theory Z, was developed by considering what characteristics high-performing organizations shared. This theory focuses more on the cultural side of the organization and identifies ten characteristics shared by high-performing organizations :

1. Trust
2. Subtlety and intimacy
3. Shared control and decision making
4. Training and planning
5. Organization processes
6. Budgeting systems

7. Interpersonal skills
8. Motivation through self-interest
9. Rewards in the long run
10. High-quality education

Finally, the superleadership theory promotes the idea that a leader's main task is to help others develop as leaders. Unlike previous theories, the idea of a sSuperleader" distances itself from the ideals of a single dominant leader found in previous theories. Anyone can learn to be a leader. In fact, everyone is, to some extent, a leader, and it is up to the "superleader" to recognize their followers' abilities and find ways to help them develop their abilities. Becoming a "superleader" requires a seven-stage process:

1. Become a self-leader by showing effective behavior, effective thinking, and cognitive abilities.
2. Modeling self-leadership by demonstrating the right skills to followers.
3. Encouraging self-set-goals.
4. Create positive thought patterns.
5. Develop self-leadership through reward and constructive reprimand.
6. Promote self-leadership through teamwork.
7. Facilitate a self-leadership culture.

Transformational Leadership Theory
20th Century (1940s - 1990s)

Major Theorists: Weber (1947), House (1977), Burns (1978), Bass (1985), Shamir et al. (1993)

The basis of the following theory is that leaders and followers are mutually engaged in a relationship that leads both parties to greatness. Leaders should try to influence their followers by inspiring them and attracting them to their values. This, in turn, should lead to followers delivering excellent results for the organization and wanting to prioritize the organization's general good. Therefore, the effectiveness of a transformational leader lies in their ability to provide their followers with meaningful work and a high moral purpose. This theory of leadership is meant to be flexible and something that can be applied by anyone, in any situation, and in any organization or industry. An important distinction from the transactional leadership theory is that leaders are inspiring their followers to gain their motivation, rather than needing to give followers what they want to gain their motivation. Like most theories, some variations exist between the different approaches.

One approach developed by Burns considered that the leader and their followers build a situation of reciprocal influence, where the objective is to help one another grow into a better self. This reciprocal relationship is based on high moral values expressed by the leader, such as liberty, justice, equality, and collective well-being. A successful leader will get their followers to embrace and identify with their values. Under this approach, four types of transformational leaders are identified:

1. The Intellectual: focuses on sharing visions and ideas that can transform society by raising social consciousness.
2. The Reformer: searches to match the means to the ends and rely on moral principles.
3. The Revolutionary: seeks to develop a new ideology, to create a movement, and to overthrow the status quo.
4. The Charismatic: tries to behave as an example and transform the needs and values of their followers.

Bass furthered the work of Burns by proving that, through the relationship built from transformational leadership, leaders are able to get an outstanding level of performance from their followers. Followers are willing to excel at their tasks because they feel inspired by the shared vision they have with their leader. They feel they are completing a mission of high importance—something that extends beyond their self-satisfaction. A leader can refer to four characteristics to connect to the transformational abilities: charisma, inspirational motivation, intellec-tual stimulation, and individual consideration.

1. Charisma: provides vision and sense of mission, instills pride, gains respect and trust.
2. Inspiration: communicates high expectations, uses symbols to focus efforts, and expresses important purposes in simple ways.
3. Intellectual stimulation: promotes intelligence, rationality, and careful problem-solving.
4. Individualized consideration: gives personal attention, treats each employee individually, coaches, and provides advice.

House further extended Burns' work by building the idea of a charismatic leader. So, what is a charismatic leader? Someone who can generate major effects for followers, such as emotional attachment, emotional and motivational arousal, enhanced self-esteem, trust and confidence, enhanced follower dedication to the mission communicated by the leader and to collective interest, stimulate followers to make personal sacrifices, and the transformation of followers' needs,

values, preferences, and aspirations. There are five processes a successful charismatic leader should follow:

1. Increasing the intrinsic valence of effort: making the effort
   meaningful.
2. Increasing effort accomplishment expectations: enhance the followers' confidence to meet expectations by showing confidence
   in their abilities.
3. Increasing the intrinsic valence of goal accomplishment: articulate a vision and a mission to increase the goals' meaningfulness.
4. Instilling faith in a better future: provide hope and faith in goal
   attainment.
5. Creating commitment: ensure the followers stay dedicated, no
   matter what.

They should also demonstrate the following two behaviors:

1. Role modeling: set an example in terms of lifestyle, reactions,
   values, risk-taking, making sacrifices, showing courage, and engaging in unconventional ideological behavior.
2. Frame alignment: be an extensive communicator, provide guidance and structure, share values and a vision for the future, communicate expected behavior.

A major issue concerning charismatic leaders is that they may not be
efficient with all followers and in all organizations, which is a major di-
vergence from the idea that transformational leadership should be universal. This leadership style would not be successful if the values and
identities of the leader do not appeal to the followers' self-concept. If
the values do not appeal, followers will not demonstrate a motivation
to work or create social connections. Charismatic leaders may not be
successful in organizations where the tasks themselves do not relate
to social values, where the rewards and punishment process are clear
and well defined, and if the organization is not facing a situation that
requires an exceptional level of performance (e.g., crisis situation, sit-

uations with a high level of uncertainty and ambiguity, context of change).

Each of these traditional leadership theories gained prominence during the 19th and 20th centuries, and some even continue to have a place in the 21st century. However, in the following chapter, I will lay out the leadership theories developed in the 21st century which are more connected to the current state of leadership.

Overview of Traditional Leadership Theories

4

Contemporary Leadership Theories

The study of leadership is constantly evolving and being updated as it adapts to our ever-changing world. Following the traditional theories on leadership, a new set of theories have emerged in the 21st century. They take a closer look at what is required for this new age, which ideas should be left behind, and which may be more useful than we think. So far in the 21st century, a myriad of new leadership theories have erupted, contributing to more confusion and bringing less clarity. Given this increasingly complex maze of theories, it has become even more difficult to identify the most relevant and impactful ones. Fortunately for us, several teams of researchers have invested the time required to extract the most important new theories from the pack. In particular, I would like to acknowledge the team of Dihn et al. (2014) and Karaaslan (2015), to mention a few, for their effort and valuable contribution. It is because of their work that I am able to discuss a precise list of the most mentioned and discussed contemporary leadership theories.

Strategic Leadership Theory
21ˢᵗ Century

Major Theorists: Boal & Hooijberg (2001), Davies & Davies (2004), Vera & Crossan (2004)

Strategic leadership is said to be essential during conditions of high complexity, ambiguity, fast-changing environments, and information overload, all of which align with the changes the world has seen in this new century. Despite being an appropriate style for times of change and ambiguity, strategic leaders should still be able to perform well when conditions are stable. In reality, an ideal strategic leader should be able to apply both the transactional and the transformational leadership styles. A strategic leader should demonstrate the following nine characteristics, which are separated into organizational ability and personal ability.

Strategic leaders' organizational ability:

- Be strategically orientated: consider both the long-term future and the current state. Manage to link long-term vision to daily tasks, the ability to see the big picture.
- Translate strategy into action: able to assess the current state, and from it, build a clear future picture. Ability to monitor strategy execution.
- Align people and organizations: encourage commitment, articulate sense-making, and ensure values are shared.
- Determine effective strategic intervention points: able to identify the right time to initiate a change.
- Develop strategic competencies: ensure that the right skills and competencies are available.

Strategic leaders' individual abilities:

- Dissatisfaction or restlessness with the present: ability to cope well with ambiguity and to envision a strategic leap.
- Absorptive capacity: able to handle and analyze a high amount of information and identify key relevant information from it.
- Adaptive capacity: ability to change ways of seeing or doing things, capable of being flexible.
- Wisdom: capacity to take the right action at the right time, demonstrate creative skills, social awareness, and interpersonal skills.

Shared Leadership
21st Century

Major Theorists: Pearce & Conger (2003), Avolio et al. (2009), Morgeson, DeRue, & Karam (2010), Kocolowski (2010)

Shared leadership has grown in popularity as organizations adopt more team-based and project approaches to structure their activities. The principle of the theory is that the "leader" is not one person, but rather a shared responsibility among a team. This is explained by Pearce and Conger (2003), who defined shared leadership as "a dynamic, inter-active influence process among individuals in groups, for which the objective is to lead one another to the achievement of group or orga-nizational goals, or both." The suggested characteristics for successful shared leadership are as follows:

- The work team resolves differences to reach an agreement.
- Work is distributed properly to take advantage of members' unique skills.

- Information about the company and its strategy is shared, including strategic goals.
- Teamwork is promoted with the team itself.
- The team works together to identify opportunities to improve productivity and efficiency (collaboration).
- Delegate enough autonomy and responsibility to all members of the team.
- Involve the team in decision-making.

Team Leadership
21st Century

Major Theorists: Morgeson et al. (2010)

Furthering the idea of shared leadership, team leadership is truly centered on a team's needs, making sure they are met to ensure effectiveness. A team leader can be identified as the person who is in charge of making sure that the full team's needs are met. A specific leader is not chosen - anyone can become the team leader as long as they take on the responsibility of completing or satisfying the needs of other team members. For team leadership to function, two criteria must be considered. The first concerns whether the leader is internal (part of the team) or external, while the second focuses on how formal they are.

Sources of Leadership in Teams

		Formality of Leadership	
		Formal	Informal
Locus of Leadership	Internal	Team leader Project manager	Shared Emergent
	External	Sponsor Coach Team Advisor	Mentor Champion Executive coordinator

Morgeson et al. (2010)

The success of a team leadership style will depend on a leader or team's ability to know what stage the team is in and to apply effective leadership styles as required. There are two major stages that teams have to go through: the transition phase (where there is a need for team structuring, work planning, team performance evaluation) and the action phase (in this phase, the team is focused on activities that contribute to the goals they want to reach). For each phase, there are suggested functions to follow.

If the team is in the **transition phase**, the following leadership functions are recommended:

- Ensuring the right mix of people are on board.
- Defining the team's overall mission, goals, and standards of performance.
- Structuring roles and responsibilities in the team.
- Ensuring that all members are able to perform their tasks.
- Making sense of the team environment.
- Facilitating feedback processes.

If the team is in **the action phase**, the following leadership functions are recommended:

- Monitoring the team performance.
- Managing the boundaries between the team and other entities of the organization.
- Challenging the team to improve its performance.
- Performing some tasks within the team.
- Solving problems.
- Acquiring resources for the team.
- Encouraging team autonomy.
- Cultivating a positive climate.

Complexity Leadership
21st Century

Major Theorists: Uhl-Bien, Marion & McKelvey (2007), Avolio et al. (2009)

The complexity leadership theory was developed to provide a solution for a world entering the knowledge era, a time that brings enormous complex content changes. This theory is grounded in complexity science theories and relies on the complex adaptive system (CAS). In the 21st century, most organizations use one of two systems to function: the operational system or the entrepreneurial system. The operational system deals with formality, standardization, and business performance, whereas the entrepreneurial system focuses on innovation, learning, and growth. Complexity leadership aims to bring the two systems together to foster innovation, creativity, and organization performance. This dynamic system deals with unpredictability and complex feedback networks with the aim to produce adaptive outcomes. Complexity leadership identifies three types of leadership functions: administrative, adaptive, and enabling. For each of these functions, clear roles and tasks are suggested.

1. **Administrative** is the bureaucratic function with the following tasks:
   - Structuring tasks, planning, building vision, acquiring resources, managing crisis, personal conflicts, and managing organizational strategy.
2. **Adaptive** comprises the emergent change behaviors under the conditions of interaction, interdependence, asymmetrical information, complex network dynamics, and tension, and includes the following tasks:
   - Interacting between agents.
   - Collaborating (alliances of people, ideas, technologies, and cooperative efforts).
3. **Enabling** directly fosters and maneuvers the conditions (e.g., context) that catalyze adaptive leadership and allow for emergence. The tasks required are:
   - Managing the entanglement between administrative and adaptive leadership.
   - Ensuring consistency between the strategy and the mission of the organization.
   - Clearly articulating the mission (described above).
   - Offering technical support that is consistent with organizational themes.

Authentic Leadership
21st Century

Major Theorists: Fredrickson (2001), Avolio & Gardner (2005), Komives & Dugan (2010), Zhang, Everett, Elkin, Cone (2012)

Authenticity should underly most, if not all, leadership theories. An authentic leader is someone that behaves and acts in ways that are consistent with their values and convictions. Influenced by positive psychology, authentic leadership is a process that draws on both a positive mindset and a developed organizational context to promote greater self-awareness and self-regulation. With authentic leadership, followers and leaders will have greater positive behaviors and foster positive self-development. An authentic leader is based on four factors:

1. Balanced processing: factual and objective analyses before decision making.
2. Internalized moral perspective: refer to moral standards to regulate own behaviors.
3. Relational transparency: present self with authenticity, share information and feelings openly.
4. Self-awareness: knowledge of one's own strengths and weaknesses and of how the world makes sense to oneself.

Cross-Cultural Leadership
21st Century

Major Theorists: Bird & Mendenhall (2016), Steers & Sanchez-Runde (2012), Wang, Waldman, & Zhang (2012), Avolio et al. (2009), Jokinen (2004)

A significant qualifying factor of the 21st century is our increasing globalization and connection to other countries and cultures, especially after WWII. The main purpose of the cross-cultural leadership theory is to help leaders understand how to work with cultural differences, especially when operating outside of their home country. Since its initial development in the second half of the 20th century, the cross-cultural leadership theory has taken on three approaches: uni-cultural, comparative, and intercultural. Uni-cultural considers management practices abroad in a single country, comparative compares the styles in two or more counties, and finally, intercultural considers how people from different countries can interact and work together.

With the continued expansion and intensity of the international economy, cross-cultural leadership has developed even further with the emergence of global leadership theories. A global leader can be defined as anyone who has a global responsibility in their business activity. They can be found at any level of an organization. A global leader should possess these three competencies:

- The core of the global leadership competencies comprise:
    - Self-awareness: understanding one's emotions, knowing one's strengths and weaknesses, understanding one's needs and drive, sources of frustrations, and reaction to problems.
    - Engagement in personal transformation: commitment to ongoing development, drive to stay up to date, desire to experience new things, openness to change.
    - Inquisitive: curiosity.
- The desired mental characteristics of global leaders are:
    - Optimism
    - Self-regulation
    - Social judgment
    - Empathy
    - Motivation to work in an international environment
    - Cognitive skills
    - Acceptance of complexity and its contradictions.
- Behavioral global leadership competencies are:
    - Social and networking skills
    - Knowledge: technical, organization, and people.
    - Experience dealing with an international context.

E-Leadership
21st Century

Major Theorists: Avolio, Kahai, and Dodge (2001), Malhotra, Majchzak & Rosen (2007), Davis & Cates (2013), Liao (2017)

Another important classification of the 21st century is its increasing digitalization and a move toward electronic/digital methods of working. As such, it was necessary to develop a leadership style centered on the evolution of teleworking. Nowadays, employees can work from anywhere at any time, far from the organizations they are linked to. This is thanks to the development of advanced information technologies (AIT) such as emails, message boards, knowledge management systems, and information systems, to list a few. Teleworking and virtual teams are becoming more common, and we see fewer face-to-face interactions taking place in the workplace. The e-leadership theory considers an approach where AIT is used to socially influence the attitudes, feelings, thinkings, behavior, and performance of individuals and groups within an organization. Continuing the streak of non-hierarchical leadership theories, e-leadership can take place at any stage of an organization's hierarchy.

An "e-leader" should consider addressing and interacting with both the whole team as an entity, as well as each team member specifically. Some of the challenges faced by an e-leader that should be considered and overcome are:

- Overcoming the obstacle of creating team cohesion, handling workers in different locations and time zones, who speak different languages, with different cultures, and creating an appreciation of trust.

- Making sure each team member is fully committed to the mission and supporting them.
- Handling team members' feelings of isolation. Davis and Cates (2013) have explained that the feeling of isolation of team members is one of the major challenges in e-leadership.
- Providing structure and norms to team members, ensuring knowledge sharing, and motivating team members.

In order to tackle these constraints, an effective e-leader will need the following competencies:

Practices of Effective Virtual Team Leaders

Leadership Practices of Virtual Team Leaders	How do Virtual Team Leaders do it?
1- Establish and Maintain Trust Through the Use of Communication Technology	• Focusing the norms on how information is communicated • Revisiting and adjusting the communication norms as the team evolves ("virtual get togethers") • Making progress explicit through use of team virtual workspace • Equal "suffering" in the geographically distributed world
2 - Ensure Diversity in the Team is Understood, Appreciated, and Leveraged	• Prominent team expertise directory and skills matrix in the virtual workplace • Virtual sub-pairing to pair diverse members and rotate sub-team members • Allowing diverse opinions to be expressed through use of asynchronous electronic means (e.g. electronic discussion threads)
3 - Manage Virtual Work-Cycle and Meetings	• All idea divergence between meetings (asynchronous idea generation) and idea convergence and conflict resolution during virtual meetings (synchronous idea convergence) • Use the start of a virtual meeting (each time) for social relationship building • During meetings – ensure through "check-ins" that everyone is engaged and heard from • End of meetings – ensure that the minutes and future work plans is posted to team repository
4 - Monitor Team Progress Through the Use of Technology	• Closely scrutinize asynchronous (electronic threaded discussion and document postings in the knowledge repository) and synchronous (virtual meeting participation and instant messaging) communication patterns • Make progress explicit through balanced scorecard measurements posted in the team's virtual workspace
5 - Enhance External Visibility of the Team and its Members	• Frequent report-outs to a virtual steering committee (comprised of local bosses of team members)
6 - Ensure Individuals Benefit from Participating in Virtual Teams	• Virtual rewards ceremonies • Individual recognition at the start of each virtual meeting • Making each team member's "real location" boss aware of the member's contribution

Malhotra et al. (2007)

Servant Leadership
21st Century

Major Theorists: Greenleaf (1970, 1977), Winston (2004), Dingman & Stone (2007), Avolio et al. (2009), Paris & Peachey (2013), Sajjadi (2014)

The servant leadership style is often perceived as more a way of life as it considers ethics, virtues, and morality for the common good, as well as organizational effectiveness and followers' well-being. While the name may, at first, suggest a return to treating employees as a leader's servant, it actually means quite the opposite. A servant leader is completely committed to serving others. They embody trust, empowerment, vision, altruism, intrinsic motivation, commitment, and service.

Emotional Leadership
21st Century

As a final note, we need to mention the importance of emotions when it comes to leadership. At its essence, leadership is a relationship, and emotions are always at play in relationships, especially when attempting to meet an organization's objectives. We can see through many of the leadership theories mentioned in the past two chapters that emotions can be at the very center of leadership (i.e., charismatic leadership, transformational, and transactional leadership). As such, emotional intelligence has increasingly become the base of good leadership. The ability to recognize both one's own feelings, as well as those of others, and being able to manage and motivate ourselves and those in our relationship, is indispensable. Within emotional intelligence, there are three interactions to be aware of: emotions within a person, emotions between persons (interpersonal emotions), and group emotions, such as within a team or organization.

Both external emotions, which are triggered due to non-work-related events, and internal emotions, can heavily affect production and efficiency. Positive events can boost optimism, which can lead to increased performance, while negative events can become the source of frustration and negatively impact productivity. In order to access emotional leadership, there are certain traits and processes worth considering:

- Leader's traits:
  - Having empathy. Empathy is defined as "the ability to comprehend another's feelings and to experience them oneself."
  - Able to display empathy. It is necessary to leadership emergence.
- Leadership process:
  - Ability to manage one's own emotions.
  - Ability to manage others' emotions.
  - Help members cope with frustration.
  - Creating shared emotional experiences.

Overview of Contemporary Leadership Theories

5

How is our World Changing?

The expression, "the only constant is change," has never seemed more true. Looking at the countless reports and articles published in various sources, it is clear that the world we live in is changing at a very fast pace. Increased complexity, uncertainty, unpredictability-these are the terms we use to qualify today's world. Change affects most parts of society, and leadership theories are no exception. It is generally recognized that the current change in the environment has had and will continue to have an impact on leadership.

Leadership skills used in the past will no longer be enough to ensure the success of organizations. Therefore, a new set of competencies are needed. Leadership theories have constantly evolved through time driven by changes in society led by sociology, economics, and information. The 21st century is no exception. To identify the leadership competencies required for the 21st century, it is necessary to review the main trends that are shaping our world. Seven major trends are shaping the world of tomorrow: the new reality of the international economy, major sociological changes, a growing reliance on technology (especially in the workplace), a growing concern for a sustainable world, the financialization of the economy, the digital transformation, and the in-creased prominence of crises.

The New Reality of the International Economy

International commerce is growing rapidly as more and more compa-nies participate in order to achieve growth. Over the course of the last 20 years, the value of international trade has been multiplied by four, representing over 20 trillion USD. The share of international trade to GDP has increased by 10 points to represent more than 1/3 of the world's GDP. During the same period, foreign direct investment has been multiplied by five to an amount of more than 1.5 trillion USD.

In the meantime, international economic power is slowly shifting to developing countries. The World Trade Organization shows that over a period of 10 years, developing countries have increased their share in international trade by 10 points. Today, they account for more than 40% of all international trade activities. Several developing countries are growing to a position in which they will lead in the international trade arena. For instance, China has grown to become the number one player in international trade, surpassing the United States. Another ex-ample can be found in India, where Indian firms are increasing their in-ternational presence through numerous overseas acquisitions of major companies in developed countries. With this increased participation in the international economy, India is expected to surpass Japan by 2030. In addition, emerging regions like Asia and Africa are expected to ac-count for a much larger share of the economic growth and world GDP as they are currently growing at a faster rate than developed regions.

Major Sociological Changes

One of the major considerations for how the world has changed is the sociological changes we've seen shifting the workplace. Some of the main sociological trends include increased interaction among people from different parts of the world and different cultures (brought on by increased globalization), an important demographic shift, and a higher participation of women in the workplace.

Human beings have always been mobile, however, in our new globalized world, the extent of our mobility has increased significantly. A recent report published by the United Nations has shown that over the course of the last 10 years, the number of migrants, mostly for work or studies, has increased by more than 50% and it continues to be a fast-growing phenomenon. The Air Transport Action Group published another report which shows the number of people traveling by air for work, study, or leisure across continents has reached four billion people?a significant increase. These reports show how much we are moving and connecting throughout the world as humans. Most businesses today will interact with people from all over the globe and from a wide range of cultures. It has become a key part of our lives.

Globalization is not the only sociological phenomenon on the horizon. The 21st century is expected to change in several other ways; namely, a population increase marked by a swelling aging population in some areas, with others expecting a youth boom. A second report published by the United Nations shows that the world population is expected to reach more than nine billion by 2050. The shift will have a different effect on different countries. Developing countries in Asia and Africa are expected to account for just over 80% of the world's population. In addition, the world's population is generally aging with a growing percentage of people over 60 years old. Developed countries are expected to be impacted more severely by this aging phenomenon. While developing countries in Asia and Africa will also experience some aging, they will account for a high proportion of youth populations between the ages of 10 and 24. These changes will, of course, affect the workplace.

Generation Z is now entering the workforce. Millennials (born between 1980 and late 1990) are expected to represent 75% of the global workforce in the future. In addition, older generations are staying longer in their jobs. The result is a higher number of different generations working together than there has been in the past. This multigenerational workforce brings new leadership challenges as all the different generations are said to have different values, beliefs, mindsets, and different perceptions and expectations of leadership.

The final sociological trend that should be mentioned is the growing number of women in the workplace. Over the course of the last century, we have seen the participation of women in the workplace increase. In particular, the last 30 years have seen an increase in the number of women holding leadership roles. The World Bank's World Development Report in 2012 estimated that women represent almost half of the global labor force. We can only expect this to continue through the 21st century.

While culture, age, and gender have always played a part in the workforce, the increasing diversity of demographics will be at the center of the 21st century workplace and should be the key to considering different leadership methods.

Technological Impacts in the Workplace

Perhaps the most obvious change that we have seen in the 21st century is the exponential development in technology, which has changed regularly and with high intensity in recent years. People have embraced technological innovations and changes to not only improve their private life but also their working environments. Not only has technology become commonplace within businesses, but it has also become a source of competitive advantage through the increased productivity it can bring employees, allowing them to work faster and smarter. Along with existing technology, computer-mediated communication technologies and emerging media technologies have begun to change how people work and interact with each other. Emerging media technologies have allowed for the development of virtual teams, which is an asset in the global world of business. Further, it reduces geographic ties and organizational boundaries, while also acting as an addition to face-to-face communication.

Another impact of technological advances concerns the high volume of information that organizations are bombarded with at an immense speed that has never been seen before. All the information comes from different sources and devices, forcing organizations to pay more and closer attention to the veracity and accuracy of found information before making any business decisions.

Digital Transformation

With the acceleration of technology development and the increased digitization of content and of information, organizations can no longer escape from the fourth industrial revolution. To survive it, they need to embrace the digital transformation. Wade and Marchand (2014) defined digital transformation as "a form of organizational change, whereby digital technologies are used to improve performance" and to solve business problems. Digital transformation, therefore, impacts business models, operation processes, and customer experience. It focuses on leveraging disruptive technologies such as the following: internet of things, blockchain, artificial intelligence, machine learning, cloud computing, and big data.

The Rising Pressure of Sustainable Development Goals

The concept of sustainable development evolved after growing concerns about the alarming state of our environment and an increasing social exclusion. The object of sustainable development is to ensure that every country and organization in the world feels responsible for implementing the triple bottom line approach, which ensures economic development, environmental sustainability, and social inclusion.

A PricewaterhouseCoopers report showed that the sustainable development goals published by the United Nations are increasingly taken into consideration by companies. More and more executives are considering sustainability as a key factor to enhance the future competitiveness of their organization. However, making sustainability a key factor of an organization is more than just making a few small changes, which is often perceived as "green bashing." Organizations should develop new business models that incorporate elements of sustainability, both as an imperative for success, as well as making a positive contribution to the environment and our society. This is also known as the "triple bottom line." Creating and adopting such business models may force managers and leaders to face a paradox where they must incorporate conflicting but interconnected issues. However, leaders should continue to make strides towards sustainability, which may require engaging with different external actors and accepting new forms of collaboration; for example, working more closely with NGOs.

Financialization of the Economy

Financialisation is associated with the idea that we have witnessed a shift regarding the view of capitalist activity which has been moving from creating benefits through selling goods and services, to increasing profits from financial activities. Epstein (2005) defined financialization in the following terms: "the increasing role of financial motives, financial markets, financial actors, and financial institutions in the operation of the domestic and international economies." Kippner (2011) demonstrated that the concept of financialization has grown in popularity since early 2000 and is stimulated by the development of new information technologies. As financialization grows, leaders are confronted with a greater pressure to deliver fast results and quick business returns.

Crisis Management and Leadership

One can argue that crises are not new and that there has always been a necessity to address them. However, there seems to be a general awareness in our current fast-paced world that they do occur more regularly and in different forms: natural disasters, terrorist attacks, global health crises, cyberattacks, white-collar crimes, as well as organizational and personal crises, to list a few. Cenk (2015) views crisis as "an unpredictable state that disrupts normal operations for the organization and requires immediate action taking." It is commonly agreed that there are different stages of a crisis that would require a leader's attention. Badhuri (2019) believes there are five stages in a crisis: signal detection, preparation/prevention, contamination/damage limitation, recovery, and learning.

In the 21st century, leaders will come into contact with each of these major changes and will need to feel confident interacting with and working alongside them. For organizations to succeed, they must embrace the economy they exist within, the demographics of their employees, the addition of new technology, and be willing to adapt to more sustainable practices.

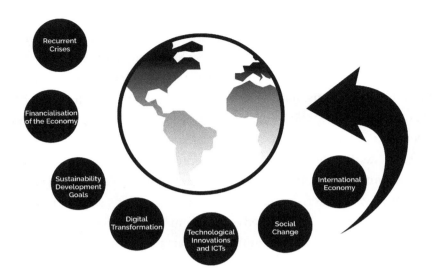

Overview of Major Trends Shaping our World

6

What is a Competence?

Before we can begin to discuss the required leadership competencies for the 21st century, it is worth defining what a competence is in the first place. The origin of the concept of a competence can be traced back to 1973 when psychologist David McClelland became a pioneer in steering away from psychometrics as a predictor of a person's performance on the job. He believed the best predictors of job performance were enduring personal characteristics. This led to the development of the competencies test. However, in 1982, Gerald V. Barrett disagreed with this theory and suggested that intelligence should not be fully ruled out. He believed cognitive ability should also be considered in the assessment of job performance prediction.

There is a general agreement that a competence is a viable concept to equip, recruit, and develop the workforce for a particular job in order to ensure success in doing the job. However, there is still no agreement on a single definition of competence. From McClelland's perspective, competencies are best described with the iceberg metaphor. People's knowledge and skills represent the visible part of the iceberg, while their underlying and enduring characteristics or self-concepts, traits, and motives are hidden under the water but represent the larger portion of the iceberg.

Other academics agree that competencies are underlying characters that result in the effective performance of a person in a job or situation. These could include motives, traits, skills, aspects of one's self-image, social roles, or a body of knowledge. Some of these competencies are visible, such as knowledge and skills, while others are not, like traits and motives.

Despite this general understanding and agreement on what a competence is, when delving deeper into academic literature, terms are often used interchangeably and inconstantly. "Skills" are sometimes used to mean "competences" and "traits" presented by some researchers are presented as "behaviors" by others. Adding to the possible confusion, the term "competence" is also written differently, while maintaining the same meaning. Other ways of discussing competence include competency, competencies, competency-models, or competency-based training.

For the purpose and clarity of this book, competencies are defined as the set of leadership qualities that will help leaders perform well in this fast-changing and complex world. These competencies include knowledge, traits, skills, self-concept, motives, and personal characteristics.

7

Required Leadership Competencies for the 21st Century

In order to be a successful leader, there are several key competencies that a person requires. While we have explored a history full of trying to define what makes a good leader, the emphasis of this book is on the 21st century and what someone should focus on today if they want to make their way into the world as a leader. This chapter will outline the competencies required to be a good leader and the particular focuses needed for a leader in the 21st century. For each competence, I will provide a suggested tip on how to enact these competencies in your workplace.

These first competencies are tried and true and have existed throughout centuries of leadership. Some have specific additions that have changed over the years to specifically fit the needs of the 21st century. Not all competencies of the past are obsolete—some of them have continued to yield positive results by adapting to society throughout every new century.

Social Skills

The first competence required is excellent social skills. As with many competencies, social skills are defined in various ways. Essentially, they are skills that result in outcomes that are socially important. The main focus should be placed on facilitating and maintaining positive social relationships. This includes developing friendships and being both accepted by and accepting your peers. A leader should also help the individuals they lead cope and adapt to the social environment they work in. Essentially, a leader should be able to connect and feel at ease with their followers. They should show their interpersonal skills and become close to people by approaching them, initiating social connections, and maintaining those connections.

A distinction that is worth noting is the difference between social skills and a social competence. Social skills are the specific behaviors one enacts, while a social competence is a judgment received from others about one's effectiveness socially.

In the 21ˢᵗ Century

The importance of social skills as a competence has remained throughout the centuries, and this is still true for leaders in the 21ˢᵗ century. In many of the past and present leadership theories, we have noted the importance of a leader that is charismatic and able to connect and form relationships with their peers. This is often how they are able to become leaders?by having a connection and respect for those surrounding them.

Social Skills in Action

- *Communication is key! Speak to people, give them individual attention, and make them feel respected. Create an atmosphere where socializing and friendship are acceptable while a lot of work can still be done.*
- *Make an effort to get to know your peers, their names, and their goals. This may also include small talk, such as asking about recent holidays or family.*
- *Listening is key! A good leader is someone who is sensitive to others and truly considers their thoughts and reactions. Take the time to listen to team members.*
- *Show your empathy: make eye contact, respect personal space, have manners, make people feel they matter, be positive and optimistic, and work together harmoniously.*

Human Orientation

This competence is closely tied to social skills. It is a reminder that, for the time being, the world has not been taken over by robots or aliens. An effective leader must be human-oriented. Human orientation considers the extent to which a leader, organizations, or even a society motivates and rewards individuals for being generous, caring, kind, altruistic, and friendly. Essentially, realizing and rewarding being human. As a leader, you should pay attention to the people you lead and have consideration for them. A good leader will focus on their followers and show interest in their development by offering feedback as well as coaching them.

In the 21st Century

The attention on feedback and coaching has become instrumental to leadership in the 21st century. Due to the continuously changing environment, leaders should take extra care to consider their followers, prioritize their wellbeing, and show more empathy for them than in past centuries of leadership.

Human Orientation in Action

- *Command both the respect and friendship of your peers. A good leader can be close to their followers while still maintaining a sense of authority and position.*
- *Be visible and available to your peers. Consider working in an open space among your followers, or keeping the door to your office open.*
- *Use your social skills to communicate and listen, show respect and empathy.*

Organizational Skills

One of the most important competencies for a leader is organizational skills. The term "organizational skills" refers to a leader's ability to organize work, distribute roles, create plans and structure, and set objectives and direction. It also includes conducting follow-ups and providing feedback. While it may often be pushed to the side in favor of more charismatic competencies, big ideas, and inspirational abilities, organization is a key competence for any leader since it brings structure and allows for clear communication, creating an efficient work environment that allows each member to know their role and pursue it with purpose.

In the 21ˢᵗ Century

In our technological society, organizational skills extend to new media and new information technologies. An effective leader should be able to organize and manage virtual teams. They should be able to show as much interest and skill with an online team as with an in-person one. Many organizations work on an international scale, due to increasing globalization, this often demands a leader to be able to manage teams of individuals, which may be spread out across the world, and to create a team atmosphere despite the inability to sit in the same room.

Organizational Skills in Action

- *Create clear visions, plans, and targets for your employees. This will allow everyone to know what is expected of them and allow them to deliver what you want.*
- *Create a clear structure for your team by delegating and dividing work.*
- *Your team is looking to you to create directives. Work will be more efficient if everyone feels confident that they are working on something important and useful.*

Adaptability and Flexibility

Adaptability and flexibility, also called agility by some authors, concern a leader's ability to adjust their behaviors and leadership style depending on the situations they find themselves in, as well as the people they are overseeing. Building on the competencies of social skills and human orientation, leaders should be able to identify and understand the different needs, feelings, experiences, and expertise of individuals, and adapt their behavior and leadership styles accordingly. While early leadership theories believed in a stagnant use of one style, this was quickly seen as ineffective. Leaders should be able to observe their environment and use whatever style will be most effective.

In the 21ˢᵗ Century:

Flexibility and adaptability have become even more important to leaders in the 21ˢᵗ century. Our world continues to change rapidly, in particular, due to the influence of fast technological evolutions. Leaders should feel confident in their ability to quickly change the course of action to be able to operate in a changing environment by providing innovative solutions. As mentioned previously, increasing globalization also demands leaders to work with different cultures and be able to understand and adapt their work styles to those of others.

Adaptability and Flexibility in Action

- *Anticipate changes and design the best possible way to quickly and successfully adjust to the change.*
- *React to a situation. Internalize and reflect upon the environment you find yourself in and then tailor plans, actions, and behaviors according to that specific situation. Some situations will require you to be authoritative, while others will require collaboration and participation.*
- *Things may often require a quick response or action.*
- *Adapt to different cultures and even age groups. Respect and see the value of different perspectives.*
- *Adapt your leadership style between your in-person teams and those online. It can often be more difficult to create a close relationship, trust, or command respect over a computer. Be flexible with how you attempt the two roles differently.*
- *Always think yes before no. Be positive about how methods, changes, or new ideas may work instead of finding the reasons they won't.*
- *Be willing to learn new methods, procedures, or techniques.*

• *Do not blame others and focus on mistakes, but instead look at what you can do to move forward and learn from them. Keep a positive attitude and always bounce back from setbacks.*

Values

A leader's behavior and decisions should be anchored in their values. Their values should guide the way they act and be passed on to their followers. Shared values in a team are important in creating a sense of community, as well as uniting goals. Leaders, together with their followers, should work towards the greater good and value the well-being of others. In addition to putting trust at the center of their relationships with followers, leaders should also be value-driven, hardworking, and results-oriented.

In the 21st Century:

The set of values that are seen as important for a leader have expanded through the years. Three notable additions for leaders of the 21st century to demonstrate are authenticity, curiosity, and moral values. Curiosity speaks to the constant changes and new ideas that leaders should be open to, while authenticity aims to create honest relationships and environments for those working alongside you and helps you be true to yourself. Moral values have become increasingly important in the workplace, especially ethical working standards and greater consideration towards doing good for people and the environment. Work-life balance has also become more essential than ever.

Values in Action

- *Commit fully to your role and work hard when you need to catch up.*
- *Trust those around you. Assume they have good intentions and forgive mistakes. Avoid being harsh or judgemental.*
- *Be results-driven. Set high standards for yourself and others around you. You should find pleasure in achieving your goals and high levels.*
- *Work towards the greater good and be aware of your moral virtues. Your focus should be on creating a positive outcome for your organization, but also for society and the environment.*
- *Be optimistic. Approach every day with energy, spontaneity, and excitement.*
- *Be curious and inquisitive. Show interest in new ideas, learning, and exploring.*
- *Be authentic. Behave in a way that lines up with your beliefs and your own goals, even if that means working against external pressures to conform.*

Cognitive Skills

Cognitive skills consider a leader's intellectual ability. This not only refers to intelligence but also their conceptual and visionary ability. Having a clear and strong vision and being able to share and inspire followers is key to being a good leader. Gottfredson (1997) defined cognitive ability in the following terms:

Intelligence is a very general mental capability that, among other things, involves the ability to reason, plan, solve problems, think abstractly, comprehend complex ideas, learn quickly and learn from experience. It is not merely book learning, a narrow academic skill, or test taking smarts. Rather, it reflects a broader and deeper capability for comprehending our surroundings?"catching on," "making sense" of things, or "figuring out what to do" (p. 13).

In the 21st Century:

A leader's cognitive abilities are also extended towards analyzing and synthesizing mass amounts of information coming from different sources with various credibility and validity levels. They should be able to then use their analysis to formulate strategies for the future. As a general, leaders of the 21st century should be strong strategic thinkers and future-oriented, both in terms of considering the changes to come and the possible challenges they will bring, as well as planning for long-term positive outcomes. In this fast-changing world, leaders need to display an entrepreneurial mindset, strong creative abilities, and be able to foster innovations.

Cognitive Skills in Action

- *Think outside the box.*
- *Have a clear strategy. Understand the challenges you are facing and consider any future challenge that awaits, and then be open to the ideas of others to help find ways to approach these challenges.*
- *Be creative.*
- *Step away from old solutions and old ways of doing things and embrace what is new and what has maybe necessarily been tried.*

Self-Awareness

Many of the competencies we have explored rely on the external actions and relationships of a leader. However, in order to be able to adjust their external competencies, leaders should first look internally. In fact, just as leaders should be aware of their followers' needs and health, they should also consider their own. Leaders should be aware of their own wants, needs, drive, and expectations. They should pay attention to what is going right and what is going wrong in their life in order to take action to improve their own situations. It is essential that they know what their purpose is and to be confident of this purpose, and therefore, themselves. Self-aware leaders have solid foundations to be more successful, show greater humility, be more tolerant of stress, and be able to overcome the obstacles they meet on their way to achieving their goals.

In the 21st Century:

A leader's ability to be self-aware has become steadily more important due to the increasing complexity and uncertainty of today's world. In order to navigate and lead a team through such complexity and uncertainty, they should be self-confident, able to handle stress, and be sure of their motivations, goals, and purpose. In addition, just as they are expected to provide feedback to their peers, a leader should practice self-reflection. Critically analyzing oneself and one's actions will allow a leader to find places in which they can improve, change, and ultimately, become a better leader. They should also regulate their emotions and behaviors, and actively manage to keep a positive attitude.

Self-Awareness in Action

- *Stay healthy, both physically and mentally. Practice sports, yoga, meditation, and eat well.*
- *Find a balance in your life that will lead you to greater efficiency as a leader.*
- *Know your limits. You cannot grow as a leader if you are burnt out and unable to perform your job.*
- *Take the time to understand why something is happening. Find the purpose within your actions and then help your followers understand it as well. "Why am I doing this?" and "Why are we doing this as a group?" are important questions to answer.*
- *Listen for feedback. Hear what is being said about you, your performance, your errors, your flaws, and recognize these. Then, reflect on how you can improve.*
- *Control your emotions in situations of stress, frustration, and conflict. Find strategies to regulate your anger, irritation, and temper.*
- *Be aware of your own subjective experiences and inner processes. Understand your thoughts and feelings and be able to articulate these to those around you.*

Transformational Ability

The competence of transformational ability refers to a leader's capacity to achieve social change. This includes their ability to be charismatic and provide a vision and mission to their followers. Going as far back to the great man theory of leadership, being able to seem heroic and gallant in your goals still remain important competencies for leaders today. The competencies should be used to inspire others, as well as provide meaningful tasks that will create passion and interest. This competence is all about what vision the leader can provide, and especially, how others can relate to that vision.

Some of the greatest leaders in history have been considered heroes while using their positions to help change the world around them. Nelson Mandela, South Africa's first black president, had a clear vision and dream to destroy the apartheid government. His visions were widely shared, and he was able to inspire those around him, which is what led to his success. Despite the hate and obstacles he faced, Mandela remained compassionate and optimistic. He connected with the public and continuously inspired a better future for South Africa, for blacks, and the world.

Similarly, Mahatma Gandhi brought a sense of direction and purpose to the Indian freedom movement. The movement existed in fragmented interest until he was able to unite his efforts. He inspired those around him with his theory of non-violence and brought each citizen of India into the freedom struggle, making each of their contributions count.

In the 21st Century:

Just as moral values have become increasingly important, a willingness and ability to bring change is highly valued among leaders. They should implement these changes by motivating others with clear goals, setting high-performance standards and expectations, and being fair and honest. Throughout this process, they should appreciate their peers and their work, and continuously motivate them to look towards the greater good of the organization and the world around them. One key flaw to avoid in becoming a heroic figure is to avoid getting lost in your own self-interests but always use your position to challenge yourself and inspire others.

Transformational Ability in Action

- *Give everything 100%. Your enthusiasm and effort will be impressive and inspiring to others. Be motivated, and through that, motivate those around you.*
- *Learn from your experiences, make corrections, and improve things.*
- *Communicate a sense of purpose to your followers so they can also act in a meaningful way.*

Communication Skills

Communication encompasses both good oral communication as well as excellent listening. Communication is at the center of many other key competencies as it allows efficient and clear interaction between a leader and their followers. Leaders need excellent communication to create relationships with their peers and to express their vision, values, and goals, as well as provide instruction and structure. Even the best ideas and intentions can fall apart with bad communication. A leader should not only be able to say the right thing, but they should also be able to say the right thing in the right way.

In the 21st Century:

For centuries, being able to express yourself through speech, in a meeting room, or conversation was sufficient for a good leader. However, the 21st century has brought other changes. New media and new technologies have brought new challenges and required nuances when it comes to communication. Leaders in today's world should be proficient in using new media and social media networks to communicate efficiently. This includes finding strategies to communicate with an international or remote team through Skype or Zoom meetings and being able to communicate the organization's brand and vision on Twitter or Facebook. In addition, given that more and more work is accomplished collaboratively, the ability to be a good listener is paramount. Communication skills should also be used to interact efficiently in a diverse workplace with different cultures and generations.

Communication Skills in Action

- *Listen actively. Make sure your followers feel heard and understood.*
- *Use non-verbal cues such as nodding, eye contact, and pausing.*
- *Use verbal skills such as mirroring, back-tracking, and reflecting.*
- *If you do not understand, ask questions.*
- *Be able to hear feedback from employees.*
- *Be productively active on social media and use it to clearly spread your vision.*
- *Feel at ease leading through a screen, cameras, etc.*
- *Sharpen your writing and editing skills.*
- *Be a storyteller.*

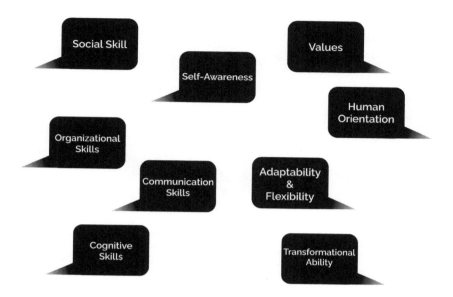

Nine Classic Leadership Competencies

8

Emerging Leadership Competencies Specific to the 21st Century

As we have seen throughout the chapters of this book, leadership is no new concept. In every era, theorists, scientists, and the general population have considered the phenomenon and found key competencies necessary for leaders living in their century. The same is true of the 21st century. With the changes in society and our mindsets, there are new specific competencies that are essential for leaders in the 21st century.

Knowledge

The first of these new competencies identified for a leader of the 21st century is knowledge, specifically in the form of expertise. This competence has become clear in the literature on emerging leadership which is paramount to the leadership theories of the 21st century. This expertise may come in the form of technical expertise, the ability of a leader to manage new media technologies, or strategic formulation expertise, the ability of a leader to choose the best course of action for the goals of their organization. Considering the importance of technology and clear goals within contemporary organizations, this comes as no surprise. In addition to technical and strategic formulation, a leader should also be proficient in capturing, analyzing, managing, and sharing their knowledge with others. As the world continues to change at a fast pace, knowledge is created and circulated much faster than it has in the past. Because of this, to stay up to date, leaders should be continuously learning and taking interest in the world and their industries.

Knowledge/Expertise in Action

- *Expertise is a way of creating credibility and legitimacy among your teams.*
- *You do not need to be an expert in every field. It is better to have good knowledge and cross-functional expertise, to be able to adapt to different functions and situations.*
- *Be open to constantly learning, particularly since things change so quickly.*
- *Sometimes you need to reeducate yourself.*

Global Leadership

One of the major changes we have seen in the 21st century concerns increased globalization. As such, leaders must be able to handle an internationalized world. They should also be able to adapt to different cultures and people, as well as be able to handle international teams and assignments.

Global Leadership in Action

- *Have an international background.*
- *Look for opportunities to work internationally or with different cultures.*
- *You must be able to understand the multi-cultural environment, as well as business environments.*
- *Be able to scale your projects. Understand how something may work in, for example, America, and then adapt the plan for Asia or Europe. Copy and paste will not work.*

Collaboration and Participative Leadership Style

While many traditional leadership theories have relied on more authoritative, top-down structures, the 21st century has adopted a more open, collaborative leadership style with a lateral structure. Collaborative and participative leadership styles are the preferred styles of leading in the 21st century. Therefore, a leader should involve all team members at all levels of decision-making. They should create an atmosphere where discussion and exchange are valued by being open to the ideas and points of view of their followers. Although everyone gets an opinion and a chance to put their ideas forward, the leader still remains responsible and accountable for guiding a project forward.

Collaboration and Participative Leadership in Action

- *Change your behavior to be more collaborative and agile so that you are able to work across functions.*

- *Be open to different ideas, perspectives, and ways to accomplish something.*
- *Allow team members to express their ideas, listen to those ideas, and respect those ideas (this does not mean you always have to choose or use an idea, but it may lead to another solution or be useful in another situation).*

Customer-Centric Orientation

The 21st century styles of leadership have taken "the customer is always right" to a new level. Leaders are not only expected to put the customer first, but they should also involve them in an organization's process by allowing them to collaborate, co-create, and become a part of the decision-making. Leaders are expected to listen to their customers and understand their needs and expectations. In a sense, the customers are the second team that a leader should work with. They should feel close to their customers, interact with them regularly, and always be looking to satisfy them and solve their problems.

Customer-Centric Orientation in Action

- *Provide training, tools, resources, policies, and a mindset for your team members to become customer-oriented.*
- *Be aware of customers' needs and wants and use them to keep the customer at the center of your decision-making processes.*
- *Strive to provide customers with an excellent experience.*
- *Pay attention to the customer lifecycle and deliver exceptional customer service.*
- *Maintain a close relationship with your customers.*

• *Optimize data and information management to optimize one's knowledge of the organization's customers.*

Digital Competencies

Synchronic literacy is an example of a specific digital competence that is useful for leaders, to be able to read and communicate photo-visual content, as well as vocal and digital stimuli. Another necessary digital competence that helps leaders create meaningful new content is multi-dimensional authentic thinking. Being able to integrate existing information, as well as not getting lost in a virtual network, are important for a leader of the 21st century. As mentioned before, leader visions should extend beyond the office and should be transferred into digital visions and strategies that include new business models. In order to successfully perform in our digitized economy, information technology should be brought into daily activities. Being a leader within this fourth industrial revolution requires one to excel at real-time action taking, being able to interact with both stakeholders and customers, and provide feedback to employees. Overall, a leader should not only be comfortable and skilled at using digital tools, whether it is for communication, collaboration, data analytics, automating tasks, or improving operations, but they also need to integrate strategic formulation into the business models and elements related to digital technologies.

Digital Competencies in Action

• *Be able to interact with stakeholders through games or challenges using social media channels such as Instagram.*

- *Change the organizations' business and operations models by incorporating digital technologies such as the internet of things, blockchain, artificial intelligence, robotics, etc.*
- *Be able to lead digital transformation projects.*
- *Be able to make customers' experience a key driver for the company's future successes.*

Financialization and Leadership Competencies

Despite the previous sentiments in this chapter that a leader should orient themselves towards their teams and their customers, putting their needs first, a leader must also consider how to survive the financialized world we live in. Leaders should be short-term oriented and apply a centralized approach to work and make decisions. This can mean they must sometimes give less autonomy to their subordinates and remain in charge. They should have a clear understanding of financial information systems and understand the science of finance overall. Proficiency in these concepts is important so they have the capacity to develop strategies and business models that are financially oriented. It is suggested that a leader be able to balance value creation activities with value extraction activities.

Financialization in Action

- *Feel at ease applying both a collaborative and a very authoritative and coercive leadership style almost simultaneously.*
- *Show a human side but be ready to take tough decisions when the results are not there.*
- *Embrace innovation, but not at all costs.*

• *Put the organization's performance at the center of all decisions.*

Sustainability and Leadership Competencies

To help organizations deliver the triple bottom line which requires considering social inclusion, environmental protection, and economic development, leaders need to demonstrate a skill set associated with sustainable development. This skill set includes the following attributes: being well informed on sustainable issues, showing high environmental and social consciousness, being able to include a sustainable approach in strategy formulation and implementation, and in organizations' business models, considering creativity and innovation to find adapted solutions, relying on collaborative and servant leadership styles. Leaders should rely on their transformational abilities to act as change-makers. This competence is one that is not only important for the 21st century, but for the sake of every century that may come after.

Sustainability in Action

• *Spreading a sustainability culture across the entire organization. Make the United Nation's sustainable development goals and the Gap Framework available to all.*
• *Always consider sustainability issues and implications in board meetings and team discussions.*
• *Be able to incorporate the triple-bottom-line in the business models.*
• *Foster innovation and creativity in the organizations.*
• *Put the organization's performance at the center of all decisions.*

Crisis Situations and Leadership Competencies

As previously mentioned, tomorrow's leaders, more than ever, will need to handle crises on a very regular basis. To do so, they will need a set of competencies that incorporate their understanding of the different stages of a crisis and their ability to foster cooperation among different stakeholders, rely strongly on a collaborative leadership style, and show a high concern for people. Furthermore, excellent communication skills, including using social media, will become just as essential as their ability to be self-aware, transparent, accountable, think strategically, and make decisions.

Crisis Situations in Action

- *Develop a crisis management plan that includes: risk analysis, an activation protocol, a chain of command, a command center plan, response action plans, internal and external communication programs, resources, and a review.*
- *Develop, design, and perform tests on emergency-preparedness plans.*
- *Consider a variety of emergencies, such as natural disasters or chemical spills, etc.*
- *Coordinate response plans to work with public officials.*

Develop and Maintain an Enjoyable Work Environment

Happy and satisfied employees will be more efficient workers. They will suffer less stress, show higher levels of organization, be less likely to miss work, be more creative, and have better and more rewarding friendships in their workplace. The happier someone is in their workplace, the more effort they will want to put in, and the greater success they will want to achieve for the benefit of the organization.

An Enjoyable Workplace in Action

- *Facilitate enjoyment at work. This can be done through social work events at the organization, such as parties, picnics, or after-work gatherings.*
- *Some organizations may also offer activities that release stress, such as exercise facilities or massage therapy.*
- *Have casual dress days.*
- *Take the time to make the people you work with feel good and happy.*
- *Show appropriate amounts of affection and care about your team members. You should enjoy helping and contributing to other people's happiness in the workplace.*
- *Assist people when they need help.*
- *Recognize the milestones of the people you work with (birthdays, anniversaries to celebrate time spent working at the organization).*
- *Celebrate the professional achievements of your team through award banquets. Have employee recognition and rewards.*
- *Provide basic needs for your team, such as food and refreshments.*

Nine Emerging Leadership Competencies

9

How to Train Leadership

Recent studies published in the USA have shown that of the $1,252 that organizations spend per employee on training, a very high percentage is allocated to leadership training and development. The budget for leadership training continues to rise at a very fast-paced. Leadership training is defined as programs designed to improve a leader's knowledge, skills, and abilities. They differ from managerial training, which seeks to improve employees' skills and knowledge in order to increase their effectiveness with tasks and overall job performance.

Despite the rising popularity of leadership training, numerous organizations are expressing concerns about the efficiency of the available leadership training programs. The general impression is that these programs do not produce the expected results and are not as impactful in improving leadership skills. The current disruptive world is helping to shed light on new leadership requirements, contributing to a growing concern in regard to the available leadership programs. The main complaints about current programs are that they are heavily based on lecture and discussion models and that they do not allocate enough time for practical practices. The programs are overly concentrated, with too much information to absorb, making it difficult for any actual learning to occur. At the same time, they are too general and do not provide enough feedback.

In this final chapter, I will hopefully provide some recommendations on how to conduct efficient leadership training programs, which are specifically adapted to the leadership requirement of the 21st century. This chapter will provide several leadership training principles upon which leadership training should be based.

Principle 1: Leadership Development is Longitudinal and Multilevel

It is important to remember that leadership development is longitudinal. It is a journey that occurs throughout a person's life. If we consider the field of psychosocial development, and in particular, Erik Erikson's theory of stage development, we see that each person, from birth to death, goes through several distinct stages of development. At each of these stages, each person will be exposed to different experiences that trigger elements that thus shape their leadership ability. Every step and experience is important to creating their leadership abilities. Therefore, simply spending a couple of days in a leadership training program is not enough to "create" a leader. These programs can absolutely imitate new behaviors or create new knowledge or allow one to gain new skills, but they should be complemented with everyday practice to maintain and keep developing those behaviors, knowledge, and skills. Furthermore, they should continue to measure progress.

Leadership development should also be considered through a multi-level perspective. This not only means focusing on interpersonal elements but also on intra-personal ones. The interpersonal elements focus on how one interacts with others, the interaction and relationship between leader and follower. Intra-personal elements evaluate the identity and personality of the individual, the leader, and their cognitive abilities, skills, and knowledge.

Principle 2: Leadership Development Should be Action-Based

Sitting and listening to a lecturer for hours is not an optimal way to develop one's leadership skills, or any skill, for that matter. Participants of a leadership program should be put in a situation where they have to solve a problem and find the best course of action or behavior. Taking on a "learn by doing" approach will reinforce their development and learning. In addition, an action learning-based leadership program is beneficial as it stimulates the development of several different leadership competencies at the same time, as opposed to teaching them one at a time. Competencies like analytical skills, creativity, communication, adaptability, etc, will all be called into action at the same time.

Principle 3: Leadership Development Should be Based on Need

There is no "one size fits all" approach. Therefore, taking leadership competencies published in academic articles or relying on leadership theories, past or present, to design an entire leadership training program, will not provide optimal results. A need assessment consists of evaluating the training needed for an organization, a group of individuals, or a single person. It acts as a starting point in designing a leadership program that fits the actual needs of the potential participants, thereby positively impacting the results of the training. When considering organizations, investigating their external and internal contexts are great sources to evaluate their training needs. As for a group or an individual, assessing their shown skills, cognitive abilities, behaviors, and knowledge within a defined context will shed light on the individual(s) training needs. The concept of need analysis relies on the idea that leadership is contextual. A given skill or ability could be proven to be more or less necessary, depending on the context, situation, or individual. When individual training is not possible, it is recommended to add some individual coaching sessions to the group training.

Principle 4: Attendance to Leadership Development Training Should be Voluntary

The theory of self-determinism suggests that participants show more motivation in learning and development when they decide themselves to do or achieve something. As we see with principle 3, leadership training is intrinsically tied to the individual; therefore, it is especially important, that participants are self-motivated. High motivation often generates better results in training outcomes. Taking this a step further, using a voluntary-based attendance policy may also allow participants to not attend sessions that focus and train topics they already have a proven outstanding track record in. However, it is always possible to learn from others and every situation is a learning opportunity. For example, an outstanding strategic thinker could develop their interpersonal skills during a strategic thinking session as they interact with other participants.

Principle 5: Leadership Development Training Should be Delivered over Several Weeks

While an intensive one-week or weekend training program may be useful if there is no other option, it is not optimal for participants to be drowned with information overload and not have enough time to process or absorb the material. As mentioned in principle 1, this will not optimize a person's leadership abilities. In contrast, sessions that are spaced over a longer period of time have two essential benefits. First, participants have more time to process and digest the new information. Second, they have more time to apply what they have learned at work or on a project, ensuring a deeper and long-lasting learning experience. An example of a good training schedule could be two or three days of training in a week at a given time, followed by another two or three training days three weeks later. The training days will provide new information and perspectives, while the three-week gap allows time to digest, practice, and embrace the material. The lessons will become actions and habit development rather than remaining passive note-taking and thoughts.

Principle 6: Leadership Development Training Should Rely on Lecturing and Practice

To optimize participants' learning, leadership training programs benefit from using several varied training methods. Presentations, lecturing, and readings are excellent to introduce a concept and provide information. Practicing these concepts enhances the learning experience as one has the opportunity to take action, reflect, and then discuss what one has done well and what mistakes were made. Practice should extend outside of the training session and continue on a daily basis.

These principles are a guide to effective leadership training, however, it is important to bear in mind that leadership development is longitudinal. Some people may have experiences that have allowed them to start their journey with leadership from a younger age, while for others the concept may be harder to approach. On the other hand, in our fast-changing world, those who have been leaders throughout their life may find themselves missing some of the competencies required to lead in the 21st century. This is what makes training leadership particularly tricky as it requires a great deal of flexibility and adaptability.

Conclusion

I now find myself having to conclude my years of research, which I've compiled in this book. I've attempted to define leadership, to explore whether leaders are born or made, to consider the history and theories that have made leadership what it is today, to examine the changes we are witnessing in our world, and finally, to outline the competencies required to be an effective leader in the 21st century.

It is clear that leadership is essential to an organization's success. In today's volatile, ambiguous, uncertain, and complex world driven by information communication technologies, globalization, societal changes, a global economic power shift, climate change, and different types of crises, leaders should be equipped with a new set of competencies to ensure the sustainable success of an organization.

A 21st century leader is expected to initiate and sustain a collaborative working environment and understand and master the digital environment. In addition, they should be able to embrace diversity, focus on customers' expectations, keep the triple-bottom-line in mind, handle fast and constant changes, and deal with paradoxical situations such as managing necessary but sometimes contradicting objectives. In order to do so, leaders need a set of 18 leadership competencies, nine of which have been around for a while but need to be refashioned to fit the current context: organization skills, adaptability, cognitive abilities, communication skills, values, self-awareness, social skills, and human orientation. The remaining nine competencies are typical to and have emerged from our modern world: ability to handle complexity, knowledge, global leadership, collaborative leadership style, customer-centric, digital competence, competence for financialization, managing sustainability, and crisis management.

Embracing and integrating these competencies into your work will make you a leader that is fit and adapted to the requirements of the 21st century.

Bibliography

Allport, F.H. (1924), Social Psychology, Houghton Mifflin, Boston.

Appelbaum, E., Batt, R., & Clark, I. (2013), "Implications of financial capitalism for employment relations research: evidence from breach of trust and implicit contracts in private equity buyouts", *British journal of industrial relations*, Vol. 51 No. 3, pp. 498-518.

Arvey Richard, Rotundo Maria, Johnson Wendy, Zhang Zhen, McGue Matt. (2006),

"The determinants of leadership role occupancy: Genetic and personality factors". Leadership Quarterly. Vol. 17 Issue 1, p1-20.

Ashcraft, Richard. (1971), "Hobbes's Natural Man: A Study in Ideological Formation" The Journal of Politics, Vol 33, No. 4. Pp. 1076-1117.

Avolio, B. J., Kahai, S., & Dodge, G. E. (2000), "E-leadership: Implications for theory, research, and practice". *The Leadership Quarterly*, Vol. 11 No. 4, pp. 615-668.

Avolio, B. J., Walumbwa, F. O., & Weber, T. J. (2009), "Leadership: Current theories, research, and future directions", *Annual Review of Psychology*, Vol. 60 No. 1, pp. 421–449.

Axtell, James L. (1968). "Introduction In The Educational Writings of John Locke: A Critical Edition with Introduction and Notes. Cambridge: Cambridge University Press, 3–97.

Baillargeon, R. (1987). "Young infants' reasoning about the physical and spatial properties of a hidden object". Cognitive Development, 2(3), 179–200.

Baillargeon, R., Li,J.,Gertner,Y.,&Wu,D. (2011). "How do infants reason about physical events". TheWiley- Blackwell handbook of childhood cognitive development, 2, 11–48.

Bass, B. (1985), *Leadership and performance beyond expectations*, Free Press, New York.

Bass, B. M. (1990), "From transactional to transformational leadership: Learning to share the Vision", *Organizational dynamics*, Vol. 18 No. 3, pp. 19-31.

Bartsch, S., Weber, E., Büttgen, M. and Huber, A. (2020), "Leadership matters in crisis induced digital transformation: how to lead service employees effectively during the COVID-19 pandemic", *Journal of Service Management*, Vol. 32 No. 1, pp. 71-85.

Beckmann H, Franzek E. (2000). "The genetic heterogeneity of schizophrenia". World J Biol Psychiatry. 2000; 1:35–41.

Best, J. (2014), "9/24-An integral theory analysis of complexity leadership", *Integral Leadership Review*, Vol. 14 No 3, pp. 254-270.

Bettin, J., Kennedy. (1990). "Leadership experience and leader performance: Some empirical support at last". The Leadership Quarterly 1(4):219-228.

Bhaduri, R.M. (2019), "Leveraging culture and leadership in crisis management", *European Journal of Training and Development*, Vol. 43 No. 5/6, pp. 554-569.

Bird, A., & Mendenhall, M. E. (2016), "From cross-cultural management to global leadership: Evolution and adaptation", *Journal of World Business*, Vol. 51 No 1, pp. 115-126.

Blake, R. R., & Mouton, J. S. (1964), *The managerial grid: key orientations for achieving production through people*, Gulf Publishing Company, Houston, Texas.

Bloom, Allan. (1979). "Introduction and Notes to Emile". In Emile, Trans. Allan Bloom. New York: Basic Books, 3–28; 481–95.

Bocken, N., Boons, F., & Baldassarre, B. (2019), "Sustainable business model experimentation by understanding ecologies of business models", *Journal of Cleaner Production*, Vol. 208, pp. 1498-1512.

Boin, A., Kuipers, S., & Overdijk, W. (2013), "Leadership in times of crisis: A framework for Assessment", *International Review of Public Administration*, Vol. 18 N°. 1, pp. 79-91.

Bolden, R. & O'Regan, N. (2016), "Digital disruption and the future of leadership", *Journal of Management Inquiry*, Vol. 25 No. 4, pp. 438-446.

Boomsma D, Busjahn A, Peltonen L. (2002). "Classical twin studies and beyond". Nat Rev Genet. 3:872–882.

Boyatzis, R. (1982), *The Competent Manager. A model for effective Performance*, Wiley, New York.

Boyd, N., Taylor, R. (1998). "A developmental approach to the examination of friendship in leader-follower relationship". The Leadership Quarterly, 9(1).

Bresman, H. (2015), "What millennials want from work, charted across the world", available at: https://hbr.org/2015/02/what-millennials-want-from-work-charted-across-the-world (accessed 02 July 2020).

Burns, J.M. (1978), *Leadership*, Harper & Row, New York.

Carlyle, T. (1869), *Heroes and hero-worship (Vol. 12)*, Chapman and Hall, London.

Castellano Stephanie (2015). "Testing for a Leadership Gene", Talent Development, Vol. 69 Issue 9, p12-12.

Ceschi, A., Costantini, A., Phillips, S. D., & Sartori, R. (2017), "The career decision-making competence: a new construct for the career realm", *European Journal of Training and Development,* Vol. 41 No. 1, pp. 8-27.

Chalkiadaki, A. (2018), "A systematic literature review of 21st century skills and competencies in primary education", *International Journal of Instruction,* Vol. 11 No. 3, pp. 1-16.

Chillakuri, B. (2020), "Understanding Generation Z expectations for effective On-boarding", Journal of Organizational Change Management, Vol. 33 No. 7, pp. 1277-1296.

Chow, T. W., Salleh, L. M., & Ismail, I. A. (2017), "Lessons from the major leadership theories in comparison to the competency theory for leadership practice", *Journal of Business and Social Review in Emerging Economies,* Vol. 3 No. 2, pp. 147-156.

Chung-Herrera, B. G., Enz, C. A., & Lankau, M. J. (2003), "Grooming future hospitality leaders: A competencies model", *Cornell Hotel and Restaurant Administration Quarterly,* Vol. 44 No. 3, pp. 17-25.

Cortellazzo, L., Bruni, E., & Zampieri, R. (2019), "The role of leadership in a digitalized world: a review", *Frontiers in psychology,* Vol. 10, Art. 1938, pp. 1-21.

Cox, J. F., Pearce, C. L., & Perry, M. L. (2003), *Toward a model of shared leadership and distributed influence in the innovation process: How shared leadership can enhance new product development team dynamics and effectiveness,* Sage Publishing, Thousand Oaks, CA, pp. 48-76.

Cushen, J. (2013), "Financialization in the workplace: Hegemonic narratives, performative interventions and the angry knowledge worker", *Accounting, Organizations and Society,* Vol. 38 No. 4, pp. 314-331.

Daigle Christine. (2015). "Making the Humanities Meaningful: Beauvoir's philosophy and litterature of the Appeal. Simone de Beauvoir a Humanist thinker". Koninklijke Brill nv, Leiden, The Netherlands.

Davies, B. J., & Davies, B. (2004), "Strategic leadership", *School leadership & management,* Vol. 24 No. 1, pp. 29-38.

Davis, R., & Cates, S. (2013), "The dark side of working in a virtual world: An investigation of the relationship between workplace isolation and engagement among teleworkers", *Journal of Human Resource and Sustainability Studies,* Vol. 1 No. 02, pp. 9-13.

Day, D. (2000). "Leadership development: A review in context". The Leadership Quarterly, 11(4), 584-613.

Day. D, Fleenor. J, Atwater. L, Sturn. R, Mckee. R. (2014). "Advances in leader and leadership development: A review of 25 years of research and theory". The Leadership Quarterly 25: 63-82.

Day, D. V., &Antonakis, J. (2012), *Leadership: Past, present, and future, The nature of leadership, 2nd ed.,* Sage Publishing, Los Angeles. CA, pp. 3-25.

De Neve, Jan-Emmanuel; Mikhaylov, Slava; Dawes, Christopher T.; Christakis, Nicholas A.; Fowler, James H. (2013). "Born to lead? A twin design and genetic association study of leadership roleoccupancy". Leadership Quarterly. Vol. 24 Issue 1, p45-60.

Diamond, A. (2009). "The interplay of biology and the environment broadly defined". Developmental Psychology, 45(1), 1–8.

Dike, V. E., Odiwe, K., Ehujor, D. M., & Dike, V. E. (2015), "Leadership and management in the 21st century organizations: A practical approach", *World Journal of Social Science Research,* Vol. 2 No. 2, pp. 139-159.

Dinh, J. E., Lord, R. G., Gardner, W. L., Meuser, J. D., Liden, R. C., & Hu, J. (2014), "Leadership Theory and Research in the New Millennium: Current Theoretical Trends and Changing Perspectives", *The Leadership Quarterly,* Vol. 25 No1, pp. 36-62.

Dirani, K. M., Abadi, M., Alizadeh, A., Barhate, B., Garza, R. C., Gunasekara, N., & Majzun, Z. (2020), "Leadership competencies and the essential role of human resource development in times of crisis: a response to Covid-19 pandemic", *Human Resource Development International,* Vol. 23 N°. 4, pp. 380-394.

Drucker, P. F., (1995), "The age of social transformation", *The Atlantic Monthly,* Vol. 274 No. 5, pp. 53-80.

Epstein, G. (2005), *Financialization and the World Economy,* Edward Elgar Press, Northampton.

Eshet, Y. (2004), "Digital literacy: A conceptual framework for survival skills in the digital era", *Journal of educational multimedia and hypermedia,* Vol. 13 No. 1, pp. 93-106.

Fener, T., & Cevik, T. (2015), "Leadership in crisis management: Separation of leadership and executive concepts", *Procedia Economics and Finance,* Vol. 26, pp. 695-701.

Forster, B. B., Patlas, M. N., & Lexa, F. J. (2020), "Crisis leadership during and following COVID-19", *Canadian Association of Radiologists' Journal,* Vol. 71 N°4, pp. 421-422.

Galton, F. (1870), *Hereditary Genius,* Appleton, New York.

Gervin K, Hammerø M, Akselsen HE, Moe R, Nygård H, Brandt I, Gjessing HK, Harris JR, Undlien DE, Lyle R. (2011). "Extensive variation and low heritability of DNA methylation identified in a twin study". Genome Res. 21:1813–1821.

Goddard. M. (2012). "On Certain Similarities Between Mainstream Psychology and the Writings of B. F. Skinner". The Psychological Record, 62, 563–576.

Greenleaf, R. K. (1977), *Servant-leadership: A journey into the nature of legitimate power and greatness,* Paulist Press, Mahwah, NJ.

Greenleaf, R. K. (1994), "The servant as leader", available at: https://www.green-leaf.org/what-is-servant-leadership/ (accessed 02 July 2020).

Gribbin, M., & Gribbin, J. R. (1995). "Being human—putting people in an evolutionary perspective". London: Phoenix.

Guzmán, V. E., Muschard, B., Gerolamo, M., Kohl, H., & Rozenfeld, H. (2020), "Characteristics and Skills of Leadership in the Context of Industry 4.0", *Procedia Manufacturing*, Vol. 43, pp. 543-550.

Hartle, F. (1995), *How to Re-engineer your Performance Management Process*, Kogan Page, London.

Higgs, M. (2003), "How can we make sense of leadership in the 21st century?" *Leadership & organization development journal*, Vol. 24 No.5, pp. 273-284.

Hudak, R. P., Russell, R., Fung, M. L., & Rosenkrans, W. (2015), "Federal health care leadership skills required in the 21st century", *Journal of Leadership Studies*, Vol. 9 No. 3, pp. 8-22.

Iles P, Preece D. (2006). "Developing Leaders or Developing Leadership? The Academy of Chief Executives' Programmes in the North East of England". Leadership. 2(3):317-340.

Ireland, R. D., & Hitt, M. A. (1999), "Achieving and maintaining strategic competitiveness in the 21st century: The role of strategic leadership", *Academy of Management Perspectives*, Vol. 13 No. 1, pp. 43-57.

Jackson, A. R., Alberti, J. L., & Snipes, R. L. (2014), "An examination of the impact of gender on leadership style and employee job satisfaction in the modern workplace", *Journal of Organizational Culture, Communications and Conflict*, Vol.18 No. 2, pp. 141.

Jaenisch R, Bird A. (2003). "Epigenetic regulation of gene expression: how the genome integrates intrinsic and environmental signals". Nat Genet. 33:245–254.

James, W. (2009), *Great men, great thoughts and the environment*, Dodo Press (Original 1880), Milton Keynes.

Jeremiah J. Sullivan. (1986). "Human Nature, Organizations, and Management Theory". Academy of Management Review. Vol. 11, No. 3, 534-549.

Jokinen, T. (2005), "Global leadership competencies: a review and discussion", *Journal of European Industrial Training*, Vol. 29 No. 3, pp.199-216.

Jonathan Marks. (m). (2012). "Rousseau's Critique of Locke's Education for Liberty". Journal of Politics. Vol. 74 Issue 3, p 694-1706.

Jorn Olsen, MD, PhD, Altamiro da Costa Pereira, MD, and Sjurdur F. Olsen, MD. (1991). "Does Maternal Tobacco Smoking Modify the Effect of Alcohol on Fetal Growth?" American Journal of Public Health January, Vol. 81, No. 1.

Kaminsky ZA, Tang T, Wang S-C, Ptak C, Oh GHT, Wong AHC, Feldcamp LA, Virtanen C, Halfvarson J, Tysk C, McRae AF, Visscher PM, Montgomery GW,

Gottesman II, Martin NG, Petronis A. (2009). "DNA methylation profiles in monozygotic and dizygotic twins". Nat Genet. 41:240–245.

Karaaslan, O. (2015), "From "Cogito Ergo Sum" to "Vivo Ergo Sum": Current Theoretical Trends and Changing Perspectives in Leadership", *Open Journal Of Leadership*, Vol. 04 No. 04, pp. 153-163.

Kellerman, B. (1984), *Leadership: Multidisciplinary perspectives*, Prentice-Hall, Englewood Cliffs, N.J.

Khan, S. (2016), "Leadership in the digital age - A study on the effects of digitalisation on top management leadership", available at: http://su.divaportal.org/smash/record.jsf?pid=diva2%3A971518&dswid=-7260 (accessed 01 July 2020).

Knight, B. and Paterson, F. (2018), "Behavioural competencies of sustainability leaders: an empirical investigation", Journal of Organizational Change Management, Vol. 31 No. 3, pp. 557-580.

Kocolowski, M. D. (2010), "Shared leadership: Is it time for a change", *Emerging Leadership Journeys*, Vol. 3 No. 1, pp. 22-32.

Kotter, J. P. (1998). "from Leader to Leader" the Drucker Foundation and Jossey-Bass, Inc., Publishers. San Francisco, CA 94104.

Kotter, J. P. (2008). What leaders really do. In Gallos, J. V. (Ed.), Business leadership: A Jossey-Bass reader (pp. 5-15) (2nd ed.). San Francisco, CA: Jossey-Bass.

Kraft, M., Kästel, A., Eriksson, H., & Hedman, A. M. R. (2017), "Global Nursing—a literature review in the field of education and practice", *Nursing open*, Vol. 4 No. 3, pp. 122-133.

Krippner, G. (2011), *Capitalizing on Crisis: The Political Origins of the Rise of Finance*, Harvard University Press, Cambridge.

Kuhnert, K. W., & Lewis, P. (1987), "Transactional and transformational leadership: A constructive developmental analysis", *Academy of Management Review*, Vol. 12 No. 4, pp. 648–657.

Lawrence, P., & Nohria, N. (2002). "Driven: How human nature shapes our choices". San Francisco, CA: Jossey-Bass.

Le Deist, F. D., & Winterton, J. (2005), "What is competence?", *Human resource development international*, Vol. 8 No. 1, pp. 27-46.

Lee T, Lipnicki DM, Crawford JD, Henry JD, Trollor JN, Ames D, Wright MJ, Sachdev PS. (2014). "Leisure activity, health, and medical correlates of neurocognitive performance among monozygotic twins: the older Australian twins study". J Gerontol B Psychol Sci Soc Sci. 69:514–522.

Lewin, K., Llippit, R. and White, R.K. (1939), "Patterns of aggressive behavior in experimentally created social climates", *Journal of Social Psychology*, Vol. 10 No. 2, pp. 271-301.

Li, Wen-Dong, Wang Nan, Arvey Richard D, Soong Richie, Saw Seang Mei, Song Zhaoli. (2015). "A mixed blessing? Dual mediating mechanisms in the relationship between dopamine transporter gene DAT1 and leadership role occupancy ". Leadership Quarterly. Vol. 26 Issue 5, p671-686.

Liao, C. (2017), "Leadership in virtual teams: A multilevel perspective", *Human Resource Management Review*, Vol. 27 No. 4, pp. 648-659.

Likert, R. (1961), *New patterns of management*, McGraw-Hill, NY.

Longmore, A. L., Grant, G., & Golnaraghi, G. (2018), "Closing the 21st-century Knowledge Gap: Reconceptualizing Teaching and Learning to Transform Business Education", *Journal of Transformative Education*, Vol. 16 No. 3, pp. 197-219.

Lunenburg, F. C. (2007). "Leadership versus Management: A Key distinction—in theory and Practice". In F. L. Dembowski (Ed.), Educational administration: The roles of leadership and management (pp. 142–166).

Luthans, F., & Avolio, B. J. (2003), *Authentic leadership: A positive developmental approach*, In K. S. Cameron, J. E. Dutton, & R. E. Quinn (Eds.), Positive organizational scholarship, Barrett-Koehler, San Francisco, pp. 241 – 261.

Maiers, M. (2017), "Our future in the hands of Millennials", *The Journal of the Canadian Chiropractic Association*, Vol. 61 N°3, pp. 212-217.

Malhotra, A., Majchrzak, A., & Rosen, B. (2007), "Leading virtual teams", *The Academy of Management Perspectives*, Vol. 21 No. 1, pp. 60-70.

Malos, R. (2012), "The most important leadership theories", *Annals of Eftimie Murgu University Resita, Fascicle II, Economic Studies*, pp. 413-420.

Maslow, A. H. (1954). "Motivation and personality". New York: Harper & Brothers.

Mayer, J. D., & Salovey, P. (1997), *What is emotional intelligence?*, In P. Salovey, & D. J.

Sluyter (Eds.), Emotional development and emotional intelligence: Educational implications, Basic Books, New York, NY, pp. 3-31.

McAdams HH, Arkin A. (1997). "Stochastic mechanisms in gene expression". Proceedings of the National Academy of Sciences of the United States of America. 94(3):814–819.

Mccann, Jack & Holt, Roger. (2010), "Servant and sustainable leadership: An analysis in the manufacturing environment", *Int. J. of Management Practice*, Vol 4 N°2, pp. 134 - 148.

Mc Clelland, D. C. (1973), "Testing for Competence Rather than for Intelligence", *American Psychologist*, Vol. 28 No. 1, pp. 1-14.

McGregor, D., (1960), *The human side of enterprise*, McGraw Hill, New York.

Morgeson, F. P., DeRue, D. S., & Karam, E. P. (2010), "Leadership in teams: A functional approach to understanding leadership structures and processes", *Journal of management*, Vol. 36 No. 1, pp. 5-39.

Mucharraz y Cano, Yvette. (2016). Leadership in the 21st Century, available at: https://www.researchgate.net/publication/304743006_Leadership_in_the_21st_Centuy (accessed 03 December 2020).

Munson, E.W. (1921), *The Managment of Men*, Holt, New York.

Nally, D. (2016), "20 years inside the mind of the CEO... What's next?", available at: https://www.pwc.com/gx/en/ceo-survey/2017/industries/20th-ceo-survey-pharma.pdf (accessed 21 May 2017).

Neha Vivek Nair. (2009). "Social Networking on the generation next". SCMS Journal of Indian Management, July - September.

Northouse, P. G. (2010). Leadership: Theory and practice (5th ed.). Thousand Oaks, CA:Sage Publications.

O'Connell, P. K. (2014), "A simplified framework for 21st century leader development", *The Leadership Quarterly*, Vol. 25 No, 2, pp. 183-203.

Okoduwa S.I.R . (2013). "Blood group and genotype compatibility". InfoHealth Awareness Unit, SIRONigeria Global Limited, Abuja-Nigeria. Vol 1, (2): pp 84-87.

Ontario Ministry of Education (2016), "Towards defining 21st century competencies for Ontario: 21st century competencies", available at http://www.edugains.ca/resources21CL/About21stCentury/21CL_21stCenturyCompetencies (accessed 30 June 2020).

Page, L., Kramer, M. R., & Klemic, G. (2019), "A Decade of Reviews on Leadership: A Conceptual Perspective and Direction", *Journal of Leadership, Accountability and Ethics*, Vol. 16 No. 5.

Parris, D. L., & Peachey, J. (2013), "A systematic literature review of servant leadership theory in organizational contexts", *Journal of Business Ethics*, Vol. 113 No. 3, pp. 377–393.

Petrie, N. (2014), "Future trends in Leadership Development", Working paper, Center for Creative Leadership, Greensboro, NC, 2014.

Petrucci, T., & Rivera, M. (2018), "Leading Growth through the Digital Leader", *Journal of Leadership Studies*, Vol. 12 No. 3, pp. 53-56.

Pinker. S. (2003). "The Blank Slate The Modern Denial of Human Nature". Penguin.

Politis, John; Politis, Denis. (2011). "The Big Five Personality Traits and the art of Virtual Leadership." Proceedings of the European Conference on Management, Leadership & Governance. p342-349.

Prince, K. A. (2017), "Industrie 4.0 and leadership", paper presented at the 17th International Conference on Electronic Business, 4-8 December, UAE, available at: http://iceb.johogo.com/proceedings/2017/ICEB%202017%20Proceedings.html ICEB (accessed 01 July 2020).

Qiu, S., & Dooley, L. (2018), "Gender Differences in Leadership Style: A Study on Graduate Students Task and Relationship Orientations", *International Journal on Leadership*, Vol. 6 No. 2, pp. 1.

Roome, N., Louche, C. (2015), "Journeying Toward Business Models for Sustainability: A Conceptual Model Found Inside the Black Box of Organisational Transformation", *Organization & Environment*, Vol. 29 No. 1, pp. 11-35.

Salas-Pilco, S. Z. (2013), "Evolution of the framework for 21st century Competencies", *Knowledge Management & E-Learning: An International Journal*, Vol 5 No. 1, pp. 10-24.

Salento, A., Masino, G., & Berdicchia, D. (2013), "Financialization and organizational changes in multinational enterprises", *Revue d'économie industrielle*, Vol. 144 No. 4, pp. 145-176.

Scandura, T., Lankau, M. (1996). "Developing diverse leaders: A leader-member exchange approach". The Leadership Quarterly, 7(2), 243-263.

Schippmann, J. S., Ash, R. A., Battista, M., Carr, L., Eyde, L. D., Hesketh, B., & Sanchez, J. (2000), "The practice of competency modeling", *Personnel Psychology*, Vol. 53 No. 3, pp. 703-740.

Sell S. K. (2019), "21st-century capitalism: structural challenges for universal health care", *Globalization and health*, Vol. 15 No. 1, pp. 76-85.

Šimanskienė, L., & Župerkienė, E. (2014), "Sustainable leadership: The new challenge for organizations", *In Forum Scientiae Oeconomia*, Vol. 2 No. 1, pp. 81-93.

Skidmore-Hess, Daniel; Skidmore-Hess, Cathy. (2016). "Have we not an equal interest with the men of this nation?" Gender, Equality, and Genesis in John Locke's Political Thought. International Social Science Review. Vol. 92 Issue 1, preceding p1-27. 28p.

Strang, S., Kuhnert, K. (2009). "Personality and Leadership Developmental Levels as predictors of leader performance." The Leadership Quarterly 20, 421–433.

Spencer, L., & Spencer, S. (1993), *Competence at work*, Wiley, New York.

Steers, R. M., Sanchez-Runde, C. J., & Nardon, L. (2012), "Culture, cognition, and managerial leadership", *Asia Pacific business review*, Vol. 18 No. 3, pp. 425-439.

Stogdill, R. M. (1948), "Personal factors associated with leadership: A survey of the literature", *Journal of Psychology*, Vol. 25, No. 1, pp. 35–71.

Stogdill, R. M. (1974). *Handbook of leadership: A survey of theory and research.* Free Press.

Talia, D. (2013), "Clouds for scalable big data analytics", *Computer*, Vol. 46 No. 5, pp. 98-101.

Terence J. Bazzett. (2008). "An introduction to Behavior Genetics". Sinauer Associates, Inc. Publishers Sunderland, Massachusetts 01375. P6-9.

Uhl-Bien, M., Marion, R., & McKelvey, B. (2007), "Complexity leadership theory: Shifting leadership from the industrial age to the knowledge era", *The leadership quarterly*, Vol. 18 No. 4, pp. 298-318.

Ünsar, Agah Sinan; Karalar, Serol. (2013). "The effect of personality traits on leadership behaviors: A research on the students of business administration department". Economic Review: Journal of Economics & Business / Ekonomska Revija: Casopis za Ekonomiju i Biznis. Vol. 11 Issue 2, p45-56.

Vallerand. R. (2007). "On the psychology of passion: In search for what make people's Lives Most Worth Living". The Canadian Psychological Association, Vol. 49, No. 1.

Van der Merwe, L., & Verwey, A. (2007), "Leadership meta-competencies for the future world of work", *SA Journal of Human Resource Management*, Vol. 5 No. 2, pp. 33-41.

Van der Zwan, N. (2014), "Making sense of financialization", *Socio-economic review*, Vol. 12 No. 1, pp. 99-129.

Van Laar, E., Van Deursen, A. J., Van Dijk, J. A., & De Haan, J. (2017), "The relation between 21st-century skills and digital skills: A systematic literature review", Computers in human behavior, Vol. 72, pp. 577-588.

Vazirani, N. (2010), "Review paper competencies and competency model-a brief overview of its development and application", *SIES Journal of management*, Vol. 7 No. 1, pp. 121-131.

Vera, D., & Crossan, M. (2004), "Strategic Leadership and Organizational Learning", *Academy of Management Review*, Vol. 29 No. 2, pp, 222-240.

Voogt, J., & Roblin, N. P. (2010), "21st century skills. Discussienota". *Zoetermeer: The Netherlands: Kennisnet*, Vol. 23 No.03.

Walumbwa, F. O., Avolio, B. J., Gardner, W. L., Wernsing, T. S., & Peterson, S. J. (2008),

"Authentic leadership: Development and validation of a theory-based measure", *Journal of management*, Vol 34 No. 1, pp. 89-126.

Wang, H., Waldman, D. A., & Zhang, H. (2012), "Strategic leadership across cultures: Current findings and future research directions", *Journal of world business*, Vol. 47 No. 4, pp. 571-580.

Whittemore, R., & Knafl, K. (2005), "The integrative review: updated methodology", *Journal of advanced nursing*, Vol 52 No. 5, pp. 546-553.

Wisittigars, B. and Siengthai, S. (2019), "Crisis leadership competencies: the facility management sector in Thailand", Facilities, Vol. 37 No. 13/14, pp. 881-896.

World Trade Organization. (2015), International Trade Statistics 2015, Available at: https://www.wto.org/english/res_e/statis_e/its2015_e/its2015_e.pdf (accessed 01 July 2020).

Wrong, D. H. (1961,) "The over-socialized conception of man". American Sociological Review, 26, 185-193.

Xu, M., David, J. M., & Kim, S. H. (2018), "The fourth industrial revolution: opportunities and challenges", *International Journal of Financial Research*, Vol. 9 No. 2, pp. 90-95.

Yadav, S. (2014), "The role of emotional intelligence in organization development", *IUP Journal of Knowledge Management*, Vol. 12 No. 4, pp. 49-59.

Zaccaro, S. J. (2007), "Trait-based perspectives of leadership." *American psychologist,* Vol. 62 No. 1, pp. 6-16.

Zaccaro, S. J., Ritman, A. L., & Marks, M. A. (2001), "Team leadership.", *The Leadership Quarterly,* Vol. 12 No. 4, pp. 451-483.

Zachartos, A., Barling, J., Kelloway, E. (2000). "Development and effects of transformational leadership in adolescents". The Leadership Quarterly11(2).

Zhang, H., Everett, A., Elkin, G., & Cone, M. (2012), "Authentic leadership theory development: theorizing on Chinese philosophy", *Asia Pacific Business Review,* Vol. 18 No. 4, pp. 587-605.

Zhang, H., Poole, M. (2007), "A Multiple Case Study of Media Use in Workplace Virtual Teams", paper presented at the International Communication Association Conference, 24-28 may, San Francisco, California, available at: https://convention2.allacademic.com/one/ica/ica07/index.php?click_key=1&cmd=Multi+Search+Search+Load+Publication&publication_id=171764&PHPSESSID=fi4u0ud92nij0m79a4g1p8gta6 (accessed 28 May 2007).

Zhang, S., & Fjermestad, J. (2006), "Bridging the gap between traditional leadership theories and virtual team leadership", *International Journal of Technology, Policy and Management,* Vol. 6 No. 3, pp. 274-291.

Dr. Guy Major Ngayo Fotso is the founder and managing director of the Swiss Institute for Leadership. He is also a Distinguished Professor of Bachelor, Master of Science, MBA, and Doctoral programs at the Toulouse Business School and the Business School Lausanne. He holds an undergraduate and master's degree in Psychology and Sociology from the University of Rouen, a master's degree in Business Management from HEC Montreal, an MBA from Thunderbird School of Global Management in Arizona, and a doctoral degree from Toulouse Business School.

He is a recipient of several awards for teaching excellence and was recently nominated for the ACBSP International Teaching Excellence Award. Besides his love for teaching, Dr. Ngayo Fotso has 20+ years of proven track records in leadership positions in major global fortune 500 organizations as a consultant for change management and a marketing and strategy executive. He has lived and worked in more than 7 countries on 3 different continents advising organizations and coaching leaders on leadership, change management, marketing, and strategic planning. Besides all this, he is also a Master World Champion in Athletics.

CPSIA information can be obtained
at www.ICGtesting.com
Printed in the USA
BVHW042102231221
624755BV00013B/863